MEDITERRANEAN DIET COOKBOOK FOR BEGINNERS

QUICK & EASY FLAVORFUL RECIPES TO ENSURE LIFELONG HEALTH
AND LOWER CHOLESTEROL. 30-DAY EASY MEAL PLAN TO BUILD
HEALTHY HABITS & CHANGE YOUR LIFESTYLE

ZOE VALASTRO

OUR FAMILY COOKBOOK

—

SIMPLE & HEALTHY FOOD RECIPES

ZOE VALASTRO

TABLE OF CONTENTS

04 DESSERTS

You can even indulge in one dessert a week! In this chapter, you will find tasty desserts!

CONCLUSION

MEAL PLAN

To balance meals well throughout the day, we offer several meals plans to guide you on this path.

One cannot think well,
love well, sleep well, if
one has not eaten well
- Virginia Woolf

Introduction

Many people associate the word "diet" with restrictions and a rigid diet that is difficult to follow consistently over time. You may have often heard about Mediterranean Diet, and you may think it is one of the many fad diets proposed by dieticians and nutritionists. In reality, the Mediterranean Diet is not just a diet program but it's a real lifestyle made of rules, and habits inspired by the Mediterranean tradition.

One of the reasons why the Mediterranean Diet safeguards your health is that it provides for the consumption of low-calorie foods such as vegetables, fruits, cereals, and legumes which ensure a fiber intake that protects from the onset of many chronic diseases; moreover, the consumption of foods of vegetable origin helps the biological activities in the body and prevents the onset of several diseases. For example, the properties of polyphenols contained in fruits, vegetables in seeds, and extra virgin olive oil, pigments such as carotenoids, and vitamins such as C, and E, work as antioxidants. Let's see first of all how it was born.

How It Was Born

In the 1950s, American nutritionist Ancel Keys observed that individuals in the Mediterranean region seemed to have a lower incidence of certain health issues compared to Americans. This led him to hypothesize that the Mediterranean Diet may contribute to increased longevity. To investigate this, Keys conducted a study that spanned 20 years, examining the diet and health of 12,000 individuals between the ages of 40 and 60 from various countries, including Japan, the United States, the Netherlands, Yugoslavia, Finland, and Italy. The results of the study supported his hypothesis, leading to the promotion of the Mediterranean Diet as a beneficial diet for reducing the risk of certain chronic conditions.

Did you know?

In the year 2010, the Mediterranean Diet was described as an "ancient and ever-evolving cultural heritage that is shared by all the countries around the Mediterranean sea, comprising of the knowledge, traditions, flavors, dishes, crops and communal spaces associated with the region." Following this dietary model implies preserving the traditional food culture, variety of life, and knowledge of locally available foods.

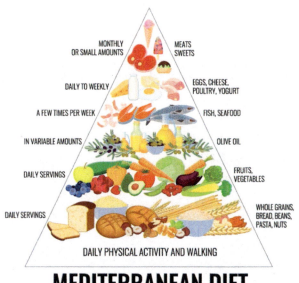

MEDITERRANEAN DIET

The Mediterranean Diet is a lifestyle, more than just a list of foods. At the base of the food pyramid, there are lots of vegetables, some fruits, and cereals (preferably whole grains). Instead, refined ones and potatoes are included among the foods to be consumed in moderation.

The consumption of dairy products such as milk and low-fat derivatives (like yogurt) should be limited to 2-3 portions of ½ cup per day. Olive oil, which should be consumed raw in small amounts (3-4 tablespoons per day) can be used as a condiment along with garlic, onion, spices, and herbs, as a healthier alternative to salt. In addition, nuts and olives can provide good fats in moderation, with one or two portions of 3 Tbsp per day.

Proteins should be obtained mainly from fish and legumes, consumed in two portions per week, poultry in 2-3 portions, and eggs 1-4 per week. And cheese in small portions, not exceeding ½ cup or ¼ cup if aged, per week.

Foods like red meat and processed meats should be consumed sparingly, no more than two portions per week or 4 oz of red meat, and one portion of 2 oz or less of processed meat per week. And sweets should be limited to the minimum.

The diet is based on bread, pasta (preferably whole), vegetables, fish, olive oil, and fruit, and provides proteins, lipids, and sugars with high nutritional value, low cholesterol, saturated lipids, and simple sugars; it is rich in vitamins, minerals, and indigestible fiber.

Fruits, vegetables, and whole foods because they are extremely rich in antioxidants have a protective action against cardiovascular diseases, and some forms of cancer. Let's see some of the benefits that bring to our body some of the most consumed products in the Mediterranean Diet.

Tomatoes are rich in antioxidants, in particular in lycopene, a substance that can protect against prostate cancer. The heating process during the preparation of tomato conserve increases the availability of lycopene making pasta prepared with this food an excellent ally for our health.

Dietary fiber is also a very important component of the diet. With its action, it prevents overeating by giving an early sense of satiety, regulates bowel functions, and modulates the absorption of nutrients, and metabolic processes. It also has a detoxifying, and anticarcinogenic action, thanks to the high vitamin contribution of the food in which it is contained.

Fish is one of the most complete foods as it is rich in proteins, heart-friendly fats, and mineral salts such as phosphorus, calcium, iodine, and iron. Thanks to its nutritional principles it is one of the fundamental dishes of the Mediterranean Diet.

The Mediterranean Diet focuses on making the right food choices, with calorie intake playing a secondary role. However, portion control and moderation are essential elements for following this diet correctly. As a guide, an adult man should aim for about 2,500 calories per day, with the majority of their intake coming from carbohydrates (55-65%), followed by lipids (20-30%), and a smaller amount from proteins (10-15%).

Our energy needs vary based on several factors:

- to our basal metabolism, (our body's energy expenditure at rest);
- what we eat (some foods require more energy to be "broken down");
- age;
- daily physical activity.

Energy is derived from macronutrients (carbohydrates or carbs, proteins, and lipids or fats), and, to enjoy a "balanced" diet, should be broken down as follows:

BALANCED DIET

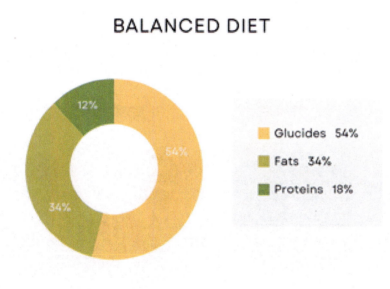

Glucides 54%

Fats 34%

Proteins 18%

- 45-60% Glucides, mainly complex (such as cereal starches);

- 10-12% Proteins, corresponding to 0.9g per kg of body weight (or 0.36 grams per pound);

- 20-35% Fats with a percentage of saturated fats (mostly represented in almost all animal products except fish) below 10%.

Did you know?

Cholesterol is a component of cell membranes, the fluidity, and permeability of which it regulates! The danger arises when cholesterol circulates in the blood in higher than normal concentrations, turning into a bitter enemy of our health.

anything else...

The most important principles of the Mediterranean Diet are contained in the following guidelines:

- higher consumption of vegetable proteins than animal proteins;
- reduction of saturated fats (animal) in favor of unsaturated vegetable fats (olive oil);
- moderation of the overall calorie share;
- increase in complex carbohydrates, and strong moderation of simple ones;
- high introduction of dietary fiber;
- reduction of cholesterol intake;
- the consumption of white meat is prevalent compared to red meat, and is however limited to once or twice a week;
- higher consumption of fish, and legumes;
- sweets are consumed only on particular occasions;
- drastic reduction in the consumption of sausages, super alcoholic beverages, white sugar, butter, fatty cheese, mayonnaise, white salt, margarine, beef, and pork (especially fatty cuts), lard, and coffee.

Benefits of Mediterranean Diet

The Mediterranean Diet allows the **prevention of numerous diseases such as atherosclerosis, hypertension, myocardial infarction, and stroke.** This diet has a valuable protective effect on cardiovascular diseases, because:

- it provides little saturated fat (the excess of which increases LDL cholesterol levels, and with them the atherosclerotic risk);
- it contains only natural sodium from foods.
- it is rich in oleic acid, which lowers LDL cholesterol without affecting HDL cholesterol;

- it is rich in dietary fiber, which reduces the intestinal absorption of lipids, and modulates the absorption of carbohydrates, reducing the glycemic-insulin surge;

- it is rich in essential fatty acids omega 6, and omega 3, which combat hypertension, hypercholesterolemia, hypertriglyceridemia, thrombosis, etc..;

- it is rich in antioxidants of all kinds: vitaminic, mineral, polyphenolic, etc..;

- it provides little cholesterol.

The Mediterranean diet **reduces the risk of developing type II diabetes mellitus** because:

- being rich in dietary fiber, it decreases the speed of intestinal absorption of sugars, preventing the glycemic-insulin spikes typical of contemporary Western nutrition;

- it is rich in starch, and fructose which has a lower glycemic-insulin index than glucose, and sucrose;

- it is less caloric than the contemporary western diet, and, since type II diabetes is frequently associated with obesity, it is particularly indicated both in prevention and in association with pharmacological treatment.

The Mediterranean diet **reduces the risk of hypertension, hypertriglyceridemia, and hypercholesterolemia**; exerting these effects are:

- omega 3 essential fats, which reduce hypertension, and hypertriglyceridemia;
- essential omega 6, and non-essential omega 9 fats, which reduce cholesterolemia;
- legume lecithins, which reduce cholesterolemia;
- phytosterols, which reduce cholesterolemia;
- antioxidants, which reduce cholesterolemia, and various metabolic complications.

The Mediterranean diet also **reduces the risk of obesity,** since:

- it is less caloric;
- thanks to the fiber, and the type of carbohydrates it contains, it has a glycemic-insulin index referred to both food, and meals, of moderate type;
- fibers promote the sense of satiety;
- it also contains a lot of water, which promotes gastric fullness, especially in association with fibers;
- it is rich in aromatic herbs which contribute to reducing the use of fatty condiments to flavor dishes.

The Mediterranean Diet **reduces overall cardiovascular risk:**

- it prevents, and treats metabolic diseases (hypertension, type 2 diabetes mellitus, hypercholesterolemia, and hypertriglyceridemia);
- prevents, and treats obesity;
- it is rich in anti-inflammatory, and blood-thinning omega 3.

Finally, it **prevents the occurrence of various cancers,** because:

- it contains few toxic-carcinogenic molecules (typical of junk food produced by fast-food restaurants). The meat of the Mediterranean diet is traditionally cooked roasted, but the frequency of consumption is so low as to be harmless;
- it provides little saturated fat, and a lot of fiber (preventive effect on the development of colon/rectal, stomach, and breast cancer);
- it is rich in antioxidants antiradical, which have a documented preventive effect on prostate cancer, and other cancers.

Therefore, while not working miracles, an eating style inspired by the principles of the Mediterranean diet can reduce the risk of developing many diseases such as arteriosclerosis, heart diseases, hypertension, diabetes, tumors (especially in the digestive system, see: diet, and cancer), and intestinal motility disorders (i.e. irritable bowel).

The Mediterranean Diet is the best in the world because it promotes a healthy, and balanced lifestyle. It allows you not only to lose weight but also to adopt a new lifestyle by eating healthy, and tasty meals, and doing some physical activity every day! It also represents a historical, and cultural heritage of great importance, and is proposed as a symbol of a cuisine whose simplicity, imagination, and flavors are appreciated throughout the world. The typical dishes of the Mediterranean diet, therefore, represent gastronomic, and nutritional excellence of the first order. The short cooking exalts the perfumes, and the flavors of all the ingredients, each of which expresses decisive nutritive, and protective properties.

CHAPTER 1 BREAKFAST

ZOE VALASTRO COOKBOOK

Health Benefits of Mediterranean Breakfast

The Mediterranean-type breakfast of coffee and milk, tea, or milk in the youngest, fresh fruit, juices or jams, cereals in the form of bread, preferably whole wheat, rusks or ready-made breakfast cereals, is rich in fiber and carbohydrates and reduces the risk of overweight and obesity, improving the metabolic profile i.e., blood sugar and blood fat levels.

The ideal breakfast must:

1. give an adequate caloric intake of 15%-20% of the daily allowance;
2. give taste, satiety, and good nutritional quality, provide vitamins, fiber, carbohydrates, and low fat;
3. include each of the three food groups:

- dairy products (semi-skimmed milk or yogurt),
- fruit (seasonal or jam or orange juice),
- cereal (whole-grain bread, toast, or ready-to-eat breakfast cereal or muesli).

"There is now a great deal of scientific evidence showing that the Mediterranean breakfast, rich in fiber and carbohydrates contributed by cereals, has a primary role in reducing the risk of overweight and obesity and in improving the metabolic profile by modulating blood glucose and blood fat levels".

Bread, pastries, but also ready-to-eat breakfast cereals-which originally belonged to non-Mediterranean dietary patterns-constitute very valid alternatives that together with coffee or tea, juice or seasonal fruit, and jam should always be present on the table every morning.

SOFT LEMON CAKE

PREP 15 MIN   **COOK 50 MIN**   **SERVES 8**

METHOD

1. Preheat oven to 340°F in static mode.
2. Squeeze the juice from one lemon and set aside.
3. In a bowl, combine the eggs and sugar and work well with electric whips until frothy.
4. While continuing to work with the whips, add a pinch of salt and drizzle in the oil. Add the zest of 2 lemons and juice and continue working with the whips.
5. In another bowl, sift the flour and baking powder. Add the powders to the mixture one tablespoon at a time and work with the whips again to incorporate the powders evenly.
6. Grease a 9-inch-diameter mold and pour the mixture inside. Bake in the oven for 50 minutes.
7. Unmold the cake and let it cool completely on a wire rack. Dust the surface with powdered sugar and serve your fragrant soft lemon cake!

INGREDIENT

- ☐ ½ cup lemon juice
- ☐ 3 medium eggs
- ☐ 1 cup sugar
- ☐ 1 pinch of fine salt
- ☐ ½ cup vegetable oil
- ☐ 2 lemon peel
- ☐ 2 ¼ cups flour 00
- ☐ 1 ¼ baking powder
- ☐ butter and powdered sugar to taste

Cal serving: Kcal: 359,3
Carbs: 48.38g | Fats: 16.32g | Prot: 4.9g | Chol: 69,7mg

CANTUCCI (ALMOND COOKIES)

PREP 15 MIN · COOK 40 MIN · SERVES 30 PIECES

- ☐ 1 cup sugar
- ☐ 1 pinch of fine salt
- ☐ 1 egg + 1 yolk
- ☐ 2 ⅓ cups flour 00
- ☐ ½ tsp baker's ammonia
- ☐ 2 tbsp butter (or 1 yolk)
- ☐ 1 cup almonds
- ☐ 1 ½ tbsp Marsala wine
- ☐ 1 orange peel

Cal serving: Kcal: 90 | Carbs: 13.4g | Fats: 3.1g | Prot: 1.9g | Fiber: 0.8g | Chol: 18mg

METHOD

1. Preheat the oven to 400°F in static mode and line a baking sheet with parchment paper.
2. In a bowl, combine the sugar, whole egg, and a pinch of salt and mix.
3. In another bowl, combine the flour and baking ammonia. Mix the powders well, then pour them into the first bowl. Mix everything together, also combining the soft butter (or egg yolk).
4. Knead with your hands, add the almonds as well, and flavor with Marsala wine and the grated zest of half an untreated orange. Knead until all the ingredients are well incorporated, then form a loaf and transfer it to the work surface.
5. Divide the loaf into two equal parts and make a long, fairly narrow roll from each. Arrange the rolls well apart on the baking sheet and brush them with beaten egg yolk.
6. Bake the rolls in the oven for 20 minutes. When they are cooked, take them out of the oven and let them cool.
7. Using a knife with a serrated blade, cut the rolls slightly diagonally, creating cantucci about 1/2-inch thick.
8. Arrange them back on the drip pan and toast them in a static oven preheated to 320°F for 18 minutes. Take your almonds cookies out of the oven and let them cool before enjoying them!

APPLE CAKE WITHOUT BUTTER

PREP 30 MIN   COOK 40 MIN   SERVES 6

INGREDIENT

- ☐ 3 apples (Golden)
- ☐ 2 eggs
- ☐ ¼ cup sugar
- ☐ 2 lemon peel
- ☐ 1 pinch of cinnamon powder (optional)
- ☐ 1 ¼ flour 00
- ☐ 1 tbsp baking powder
- ☐ 2 Tbsp sunflower seed oil
- ☐ ½ cup milk
- ☐ powdered sugar for dusting

Cal serving:
Kcal: 259
Carbs: 34.6g
Fats: 10.9g
Prot: 5.6g

METHOD

1. Preheat the oven to 350°F.
2. Wash and cut the apples, then remove the core and cut the segments into thin slices.
3. In a bowl, whisk the eggs with an electric mixer, gradually adding the sugar, then the lemon zest, cinnamon powder (if you desire), flour, baking powder, and finally the seed oil and milk. Continue working until the dough is smooth and homogeneous.
4. Grease a mold 8-inch in diameter with seed oil, then lightly flour it. Pour about one and a half ladles of dough inside and spread most of the apples on top.
5. Cover the apples with the remaining batter, level with a spatula, and garnish with the remaining apples.
6. Bake in the oven for about 40 minutes. Once baked, take it out of the oven and let it cool in the mold before unmolding.
7. Sprinkle with powdered sugar and serve!

PREP 15 MIN

COOK 45 MIN

SERVES 6

INGREDIENT

- ☐ 3 eggs
- ☐ ¾ sugar
- ☐ ½ cup sunflower seed oil
- ☐ ½ cup white yogurt (unsweetened)
- ☐ 2 ½ cup flour 00
- ☐ ½ cup cornstarch
- ☐ 1 tsp baking powder
- ☐ 1 lemon peel
- ☐ powdered sugar to taste

Cal serving:
Kcal: 479
Carbs: 73.3g
Fats: 16.4g
Prot: 9.8g
Fiber: 1.4g
Chol: 122mg

YOGURT CAKE

METHOD

1. Preheat the oven to 340°F in static mode and line an 8-inch-diameter cake pan with baking paper.
2. In a bowl, combine the eggs and sugar and beat with electric whips for about 5 minutes until light and fluffy.
3. With the whips in action, slowly pour in the seed oil and continue whisking.
4. Add the white yogurt, flour, cornstarch, baking powder, and grated lemon zest. Continue whisking until the mixture is smooth and homogeneous with no lumps.
5. Transfer the mixture to the cake pan and bake in the oven for about 45 minutes.
6. Take the cake out of the oven and let it cool, then unmold it on a wire rack.
7. Dust with powdered sugar and serve.

BAKED EGGS IN TOMATO SAUCE

PREP 10 MIN   **COOK 30 MIN**   **SERVES 2-4**

INGREDIENT

- ☐ 1 blond onion
- ☐ extra virgin olive oil to taste
- ☐ 1 ½ cup tomato puree
- ☐ 1 pinch of fine salt
- ☐ black pepper to taste
- ☐ 4 eggs
- ☐ chopped parsley to garnish

METHOD

1. Peel and slice the onion.
2. Heat a little oil in a nonstick pan, add the onion and let it brown for a few minutes, then pour in the tomato puree.
3. Season with salt and pepper, mix, and cook on low heat for 15-20 minutes.
4. After the cooking time has elapsed, create 4 small spaces in the sauce and break the eggs inside them. Cover with a lid and cook for 5 minutes.
5. Sprinkle the eggs with fresh parsley and serve hot.

Cal serving: Kcal: 188 | Carbs: 4.5g | Fats: 15.1g | Prot: 8.8g | Fiber: 2g | Chol: 204mg

FIG CROSTINI

PREP 15 MIN   COOK 5 MIN   SERVES 4

- ☐ 2 slices rye bread
- ☐ 2 figs
- ☐ 1 cup goat ricotta cheese
- ☐ 2 tbsps heavy cream
- ☐ fine salt to taste
- ☐ black pepper to taste
- ☐ a drizzle of extra-virgin olive oil
- ☐ 6 walnut kernels
- ☐ wild fennel to taste

Cal serving: Kcal: 146 | Carbs: 17.1g | Fats: 2.6g | Prot: 5.4g | Fiber: 2.4g | Chol: 18mg

METHOD

1. Cut the bread slices in half and toast them on a hot griddle.
2. Wash and dry the figs, cut off the top and divide each half into 6 wedges until you have 12 fig slices.
3. In a blender, pour the ricotta and cream and season with pepper and salt. Blend everything to obtain a smooth cream.
4. Transfer the cream to a piping bag without a nozzle and squeeze it over the toasted croutons, then lay 3 slices of figs on each crouton, arranging them on top of the cream.
5. Garnish with walnuts and fennel. Season with a pinch of salt and pepper, and a drizzle of extra virgin olive oil, and serve.

INGREDIENTS

- ☐ 4 cups flour 00
- ☐ 1 tsp fine salt
- ☐ ½ cup extra-virgin olive oil
- ☐ 1 ½ tsp baking soda
- ☐ ¾ cup water

ROMAGNA PIADINA

METHOD

1. In a bowl, mix the flour, salt, oil, and baking soda. Start mixing and add the water in 3 parts, then transfer the mixture to the work surface and continue working until the dough is uniform.
2. Form a ball, wrap it in plastic wrap, and let it rest for 30 minutes.
3. After the resting time has elapsed, take the dough and knead it, giving it the shape of a roll.
4. Divide the roll into 6 equal parts, then form 6 balls. Cover the balls with a cotton cloth and let them rest for another 30 minutes.
5. Lightly flour the work surface and roll out the balls with a rolling pin until about 1/10" thick.
6. Heat a very hot griddle and lay a piadina on top. Cook for 2 minutes per side and set aside. Continue cooking the other piadinas in the same way.
7. You can stuff the piadinas with ham, mozzarella, tomato, or whatever you prefer!

Cal serving: Kcal: 488| Carbs: 65.1g | Fats: 21.2g | Prot: 9.2g

Curiosity...

The original version of Romagna Piadina (**Romagna-style flat bread**) involves the use of lard. In the vegetarian version, lard is replaced with oil.

CHAPTER 2
APPETIZER

SIMPLE & HEALTHY FOOD RECIPES

ZOE VALASTRO

CAPRESE BRUSCHETTA

 PREP 10 MIN COOK 5 MIN SERVES 4

INGREDIENT

- [ ] 4 slices bread
- [ ] 1 garlic clove (optional)
- [ ] 1 cup buffalo mozzarella
- [ ] 10 cherry tomatoes
- [ ] 12 black olives
- [ ] 8 basil leaves
- [ ] 2 pinches oregano
- [ ] extra-virgin olive oil to taste
- [ ] fine salt to taste

METHOD

1. Cut 4 slices of bread about 1 inch thick and toast them on both sides under the oven grill or on a nonstick pan.
2. When they are golden brown take, rub the garlic clove on the bread slices.
3. Cut the buffalo mozzarella into pieces and let them drain in a bowl.
4. Cut the cherry tomatoes into four pieces, then pour them into the bowl with the mozzarella. Also add the black olives, basil chopped with your fingers, oregano, extra virgin olive oil, and a pinch of salt and mix well.
5. Arrange the toasted bread slices on a serving plate and top each slice with the Caprese salad.
6. Drizzle the Caprese bruschetta with a little extra virgin olive oil and serve.

Cal serving: Kcal: 442| Carbs: 35.2g | Fats: 26.6g | Prot: 15.5g | Fiber: 3.2g | Chol: 35mg

CAPONATA

INGREDIENT

- ☐ 1 ¾ oz pine nuts
- ☐ 1 lb celery
- ☐ ½ lb white onions
- ☐ 2 ¼ lbs eggplants
- ☐ ½ lb cluster tomatoes
- ☐ Extra virgin olive oil to taste
- ☐ 1 ¾ oz salted capers
- ☐ ½ lb green olives in brine
- ☐ ¼ cup white wine vinegar
- ☐ 2 ½ tbsp tomato paste
- ☐ ⅓ cup sugar
- ☐ Fine salt to taste
- ☐ Basil to taste

METHOD

1. Heat a frying pan and toast the pine nuts for a few minutes until golden brown and set aside.
2. Peel the celery and cut it into rounds. Peel the onion and slice it finely.
3. Wash and dry both eggplant and tomatoes. Peel them and then cut them into pieces about 1 inch thick.
4. In a pan, pour 3 fingers of olive oil and heat it. Pour in the eggplants a little at a time and fry them for a few minutes. Once they are golden brown, drain with a skimmer and lay them on a tray lined with paper towels to remove excess oil, then set aside.
5. In a large saucepan, pour in a round of olive oil, heat it, and then add onion and celery and sauté well. Finally add the capers, tomatoes, olives, and toasted pine nuts. Sauté for a few moments, then cover with the lid and cook on a gentle flame for 15-20 minutes.
6. In a bowl, pour the vinegar, tomato paste, and sugar and mix well with a teaspoon.
7. When the sauce has finished cooking, season it with salt and with the sauce you have just prepared. Stir, raise the flame, and stir until the hint of vinegar has evaporated.
8. Turn off the flame, add the fried eggplant and basil and stir everything well. Transfer the caponata to an ovenproof dish and enjoy it warm or cold accompanied by slices of toasted bread.

Cal serving: Kcal: 553 | Carbs: 31.7g | Fats: 42.7g | Prot: 10.3g | Fiber: 10.9g

INGREDIENT

- [ ] 1 cup water
- [ ] 2 tbsp fresh brewer's yeast
- [ ] 5 cups flour 00 or semolina flour
- [ ] 1 tbsp fine salt
- [ ] 2 tsp sugar
- [ ] 17 oz San Marzano tomatoes
- [ ] 10-15 cherry tomatoes
- [ ] oregano to taste
- [ ] baresane olives to taste
- [ ] fine salt to taste
- [ ] extra-virgin olive oil to taste

Cal serving: Kcal: 388,5 | Carbs: 65.5g |
Fats: 96g | Prot: 8.58g

BARI-STYLE FOCACCIA

PREP 3 HOURS   COOK 25 MIN   SERVES 6

METHOD

1. In a bowl, pour 1 ¾ oz warm water, then add the brewer's yeast and dissolve it with a teaspoon.
2. Pour the flour onto a worktop. With your hands make a hole in the center of the flour, pour in the yeast mixture, and start kneading. Then add the salt and add the remaining water. Knead well with your hands until the mixture is smooth. Also, add the sugar and continue kneading. When you have obtained a smooth dough, give it a spherical shape, dust it with a little flour, and cover it with a clean cotton cloth. Let the dough rise for an hour away from drafts.
3. Meanwhile, wash the tomatoes well, cut them up, and crush them in a bowl.
4. Grease a large baking pan with plenty of oil (4 tbsp), transfer the dough inside the pan, and gently mash it with your hands to spread it out, then make holes with your fingers.
5. Drizzle the dough with olive oil, and add crushed tomatoes, halved cherry tomatoes, and olives on top. Season with salt and oregano and let rise for 1 1/2 hours.
6. Preheat the oven to 480°F in static mode and bake the focaccia for 25 to 30 minutes.
7. Remove from the oven and serve your Bari-Style focaccia warm or lukewarm.

BARI-STYLE FOCACCIA COOKING TIPS

1 A softer focaccia

There are several variations in the preparation of bari-style focaccia. For example, to make a softer focaccia you can add a boiled potato to the dough.

2 Decrease the amount of yeast

If you have yeast intolerances, you can decrease the amount of yeast but increase the rising time.
For a more digestible flatbread, you can put only 1 tsp of brewer's yeast and, after kneading, let it rise for at least 6 hours.

3 Juicy tomatoes

If the tomatoes are not very juicy, you can add a tiny bit of water.

4 Perfect cooking

If you have an electric oven and want perfect baking, we recommend baking the focaccia for the first 15 minutes on the bottom of the oven and then moving it to the first rack to finish baking.

5 Storage

Bari-style focaccia can be stored at room temperature under a glass cloche, for 1-2 days.

OCTOPUS SALAD

PREP 15 MIN

COOK 45 MIN

SERVES 4

INGREDIENT

- [ ] 1 carrot
- [ ] 1 rib celery
- [ ] 2 bay leaves
- [ ] fine salt to taste

- [ ] ground black pepper to taste
- [ ] 2 ¼ lbs octopus
- [ ] 2 tbsp lemon juice
- [ ] ⅓ cup chopped parsley
- [ ] 2 ½ tbsp extra-virgin olive oil

METHOD

1. Peel the carrot and cut it into coarse pieces. Chop the celery into pieces as well.
2. Heat a pot full of water, and add the carrot and celery pieces, bay leaves, salt, and pepper.
3. When the water boils, dip the octopus tentacles 4 times to curl them. When the tentacles are curled, completely submerge the octopus in the pot and cook covered over medium heat for 40-45 minutes.
4. Let the octopus cool before removing it from the pot, then transfer it to a cutting board and begin cutting it.
5. Remove the eyes and central beak, then cut off the head and drain it. Cut the tentacles into pieces about 1 inch. Cut the head into pieces as well and pour everything into a bowl.
6. In a bowl, combine the lemon juice, parsley, and olive oil and emulsify with a fork.
7. Pour the dressing over the octopus, and mix well. Your octopus salad is ready to serve.

Calories per serving: Kcal: 205| Carbs: 5.5g | Fats: 2.6g | Prot: 37.2g

HUMMUS

PREP 15 MIN   **COOK 0 MIN**   **SERVES 4**

INGREDIENT

- ☐ 1 lb precooked chickpeas
- ☐ ⅓ cup lemon juice
- ☐ ¼ cup tahini
- ☐ ¼ cup extra-virgin olive oil
- ☐ fine salt to taste
- ☐ 1 garlic clove (optional)
- ☐ water to taste
- ☐ sweet paprika to taste
- ☐ black pepper to taste
- ☐ extra virgin olive oil to taste
- ☐ parsley to taste

METHOD

1. Drain and rinse the precooked chickpeas, then transfer them to a blender.
2. Add the lemon juice, tahini, oil, salt, and garlic.
3. Mix until you get the consistency you prefer: a rustic or smooth mixture, adding 2-3 tablespoons of water if needed.
4. Transfer the hummus to a bowl and garnish with paprika, pepper, a drizzle of oil, and chopped parsley.
5. Enjoy your hummus accompanied by crackers, toast, pita bread, and carrot and cucumber sticks.

Cal serving: Kcal: 507,87 | Carbs: 25g | Fats: 27g | Prot: 17.55g

STUFFED FIGS

PREP 10 MIN   **COOK 0 MIN**   **SERVES 4**

INGREDIENT

- ☐ 4 figs
- ☐ ¾ robiola cheese
- ☐ lemon balm q.b.
- ☐ Extra virgin olive oil to taste
- ☐ 1 lime zest
- ☐ fine salt to taste
- ☐ black pepper to taste
- ☐ 4 raw ham slices

METHOD

1. Gently wash and dry the figs. Then use a knife to cut them at the top to divide them into four parts as if they were the petals of a flower. Arrange the figs on a serving plate and set them aside.

2. In a bowl, mix the robiola cheese with the lemon balm leaves, a tablespoon of olive oil, lime zest, salt, and pepper, and process with a fork until smooth.

3. Transfer the cream to a pastry bag, then squeeze a dollop of robiola cream over each fig and lay a rolled slice of raw ham on top.

4. Garnish with lemon balm leaves, a sprinkle of black pepper, lime zest, and a drizzle of olive oil. Your stuffed figs are ready to be served!

Cal serving: Kcal: 179| Carbs: 7.1g | Fats: 12.3g | Prot: 10g | Fiber: 1.4g | Chol: 32mg

EGGPLANT ROLLS

INGREDIENT

- ☐ 1 garlic clove
- ☐ 2 Tbsp extra-virgin olive oil
- ☐ ¾ cup tomato puree
- ☐ fine salt to taste
- ☐ black pepper to taste
- ☐ 1 pinch oregano
- ☐ 4 slices long eggplant
- ☐ ½ cup mozzarella cheese
- ☐ 15 pitted taggiasca olives
- ☐ 4 basil leaves

METHOD

1. Heat the oil in a small saucepan, add a clove of garlic, and sauté for 5 minutes over low heat.
2. When the oil has been seasoned, remove the garlic clove, pour in the tomato puree, season with salt, pepper, and a pinch of oregano, and cook for 15 minutes.
3. Meanwhile, wash the eggplant and cut it into 4 slices about 0.4-inch thick. Heat a griddle well and grill the eggplant slices on both sides, then transfer them to a plate and set aside.
4. Preheat the oven to 350°F in static mode.
5. Break up the mozzarella cheese and compose the rolls. Spread a layer of tomato on the surface of the eggplants, and add some mozzarella, a few olives, and a basil leaf. Roll up the eggplants and lay them in a small baking dish with the top facing down. Finally, top the roulades with a little tomato sauce and a few pieces of mozzarella cheese.
6. Transfer the dish to the oven and bake the rolls for about 10 minutes. Enjoy your eggplant rolls hot and stringy!

Cal serving: Kcal: 123 | Carbs: 3.2g | Fats: 9.6g | Prot: 5.9g | Fiber: 1.9g | Chol: 11mg

PREP 5 MIN

COOK 15 MIN

SERVES 3

INGREDIENT

- [ ] 4 mozzarella cheese
- [ ] cherry tomatoes
- [ ] extra-virgin olive oil to taste
- [ ] fine salt to taste
- [ ] black pepper to taste
- [ ] 1 pinch oregano
- [ ] Some basil leaves

STUFFED MOZZARELLA

METHOD

1. Cut out the calotte of each mozzarella so that a hollow is formed.
2. Cube the tops, drain the inside of the mozzarella and place the pieces in a bowl
3. Wash and quarter the tomatoes and pour them into the bowl with the shredded mozzarella.
4. Season with olive oil, salt, pepper, dried oregano, and fresh basil leaves.
5. Stir to season and stuff the mozzarellas with this filling.
6. Garnish with a few basil leaves.
7. Your stuffed mozzarellas are ready to be served!

Cal serving: Kcal: 376 | Carbs: 3.1g | Fats: 19.7g |
Prot: 24.2g | Fiber: 1.1g | Chol: 58mg

INGREDIENT

- ☐ 4 bread slices
- ☐ 5 strands chives
- ☐ 1 cup robiola cheese
- ☐ fine salt to taste
- ☐ pepper to taste
- ☐ 4 figs
- ☐ 2 Tbsp acacia honey
- ☐ 8 raw ham slices

Cal serving:
Kcal: 417
Carbs: 41.6g
Fats: 18.6g
Prot:20.8g
Fiber: 2.2g
Chol: 63mg

FIGS BRUSCHETTA

PREP 10 MIN   COOK 5 MIN   SERVES 4

METHOD

1. Heat a grill and toast the bread slices for about 2-3 minutes per side. Then set the toasted bread aside.
2. Rinse the chives, chop them finely, and put them in a bowl. Add the robiola cheese, salt, and pepper, and mix well.
3. Rinse the figs, cut them in half, and each half into three parts.
4. Brush them with honey all over the surface and grill them for a few seconds on each side.
5. Compose the bruschetta: spread the robiola cream on the slices of bread, lay two slices of prosciutto in the center of each slice of bread, and place the honeyed fig slices around them.
6. Serve immediately and enjoy your bruschetta with robiola, raw ham, and figs!

ZUCCHINI ROLLS

🕐 **PREP 10 MIN**   ⧗ **COOK 10 MIN**   👥 **SERVES 12**

INGREDIENT

- ☐ 2 zucchini
- ☐ ½ cup robiola cheese
- ☐ chives to taste
- ☐ fine salt to taste
- ☐ pepper to taste
- ☐ 12 raw ham slices

METHOD

1. Wash the zucchini and trim them on both sides. Cut them into 12 slices 1/8 inch thick.
2. Grease a grill and heat it, then lay the zucchini slices on it and grill them for about 5 minutes per side. Then transfer the grilled zucchini to a tray.
3. In a bowl, combine the robiola cheese, salt, pepper, and chopped chives and mix well with a fork.
4. Spread the zucchini on a cutting board and sprinkle the entire surface with the cream cheese.
5. Add a slice of raw ham and roll it up. Serve and enjoy!

Cal serving: Kcal: 181 | Carbs: 1.6g | Fats: 13.2g | Prot: 13.9g | Fiber: 0.8g | Chol: 44mg

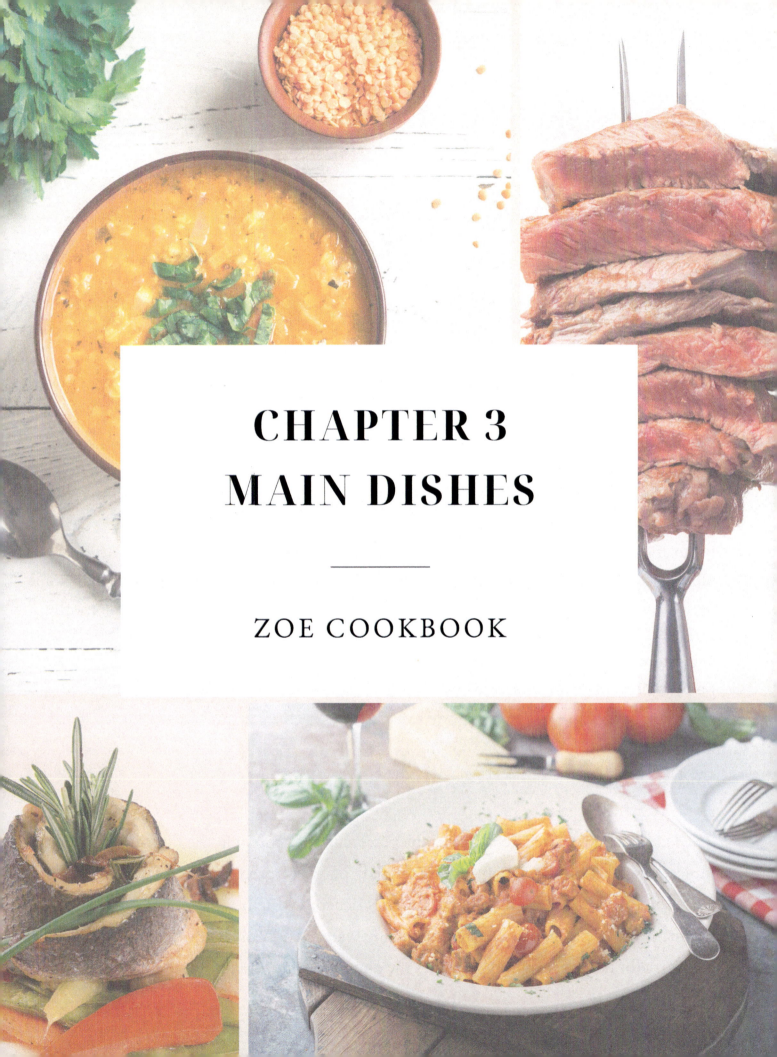

CHAPTER 3
MAIN DISHES

ZOE COOKBOOK

Cereals: the basis of the Mediterranean Diet

Cereals are the basis of the Mediterranean diet. They are versatile and lend themselves well to countless preparations. Cereals are an important source of the energy we need to live our days to the fullest. For this reason, they should never be missing from a healthy and balanced diet because they provide numerous benefits. They serve an important probiotic, hypoglycemic, and natural cholesterol control function. They thus help us prevent heart and cardiovascular diseases.

As in anything, excesses are bad for you. Excessive consumption of grains has negative effects. Excessive intake of complex carbohydrates causes them to accumulate as sugars in the bloodstream, creating a condition of hypercholesterolemia.

Therefore, it is very important to follow a balanced diet without exceeding the quantities.

Did you know?

The letter W on the package indicates the percentage of protein in the flour. A low value indicates weak flour, generally recommended for sweet preparations. A high value is more suitable for leavened doughs because it is richer in gluten.

Gluten is a protein that is activated by mixing water and flour. It forms an elastic mesh necessary for natural leavening. It makes the dough elastic and allows it to rise and bake.

PASTA COOKING TIPS

1 How to cook pasta

For excellent pasta cooking you must first bring the water to a boil, then add the salt, and finally the pasta and cook for the time indicated on the package.

2 When add salt

Salt should be added when the water comes to a boil. Adding coarse salt starting with cold water not only delays reaching 225°F but may leave an iron aftertaste to the pasta.

3 Cooking time

Pasta cooking times usually range from 9 to 12 minutes. If you use whole wheat pasta, the cooking time will increase. If you use fresh pasta they decrease (about 5 minutes).

4 Choose the type of pasta

The sauce should be chosen according to the size of the pasta, and the pasta should be sautéed in the sauce before serving. Long pasta? Choose liquid and creamy sauces. Short, medium-sized pasta? Goes well with fuller-bodied sauces (special the ribbed pasta to absorb the sauce). Spiral pasta? Great with tomato sauce.

5 Best quality

Prefer 100% Italian durum wheat re-milled semolina pasta, preferably bronze drawn. Whole wheat pasta is also excellent, rich in fiber and mineral salts.

PREP 20 MIN

COOK 20 MIN

SERVES 4

SPAGHETTI WITH CLAMS

INGREDIENT

- ☐ 2 ¼ lbs clams
- ☐ coarse salt to taste
- ☐ 1 small bunch parsley
- ☐ 1 garlic clove
- ☐ extra-virgin olive oil to taste
- ☐ ¾ lb spaghetti
- ☐ black pepper to taste
- ☐ fine salt to taste

METHOD

1. Remove clams with broken or open shells. Shake remaining clams to release sand, healthy ones will remain closed. Rinse clams in a colander placed over a bowl. Add coarse salt and soak for 2-3 hours to remove sand.
2. Chop the parsley and keep it aside.
3. Heat some oil in a frying pan and add a clove of garlic.
4. Drain the clams well, rinse them and plunge them into the hot pan. Cover with a lid and let them cook for a few minutes over high heat. Shake the pan occasionally until they have opened completely.
5. Once open, turn off the heat, remove the garlic, and set the clams aside, leaving only their juices in the pan.
6. Boiling the spaghetti in a pot filled with salted water, midway through the cooking process, move the spaghetti to a pan containing the clam juice and finish cooking by adding some of the cooking water if necessary.
7. When cooked, add the clams and chopped parsley. Fry for a few seconds and serve! Enjoy!

Cal serving: Kcal: 420 | Carbs: 67.8g | Fats: 9.4g | Prot: 15.9g | Fiber: 3g | Chol: 31mg

INGREDIENT

- ☐ 2 ¼ tbsp extra-virgin olive oil
- ☐ 1 garlic clove
- ☐ 28 oz peeled tomatoes
- ☐ fine salt to taste
- ☐ ¾ lb spaghetti
- ☐ fresh basil leaves to taste

 For more information on how to cook pasta see the tips in the "Pasta Cooking Tips" section at the beginning of the chapter!

Cal serving:
Kcal: 414
Carbs: 72.6g
Fats: 8.8g
Prot: 11.2g
Fiber: 4.1g

SPAGHETTI WITH TOMATO SAUCE

 PREP 10 MIN   COOK 60 MIN   SERVES 4

METHOD

1. Pour the extra-virgin olive oil into a frying pan with the garlic clove, peeled, and cut in half. Brown the garlic for 2 minutes, then add the peeled tomatoes and season with salt.
2. Cook covered for at least 1 hour over very low heat, stirring occasionally. (The sauce should simmer gently).
3. Discard the garlic and strain the tomatoes through a sieve. Pour the sauce back into the pan and add the basil leaves.
4. Meanwhile, bring the water to a boil in a large pot. When it boils add the salt and pasta and cook for the cooking time listed on the package.
5. Remove pasta from boiling water and add it directly to the sauce. Toss over high heat until well combined.
6. Plate your spaghetti, garnish with a few leaves of fresh basil and serve!

MEDITERRANEAN PASTA

PREP 20 MIN   COOK 60 MIN   SERVES 4

INGREDIENT

- ☐ 2 cluster tomatoes
- ☐ 1 drizzle Extra-virgin olive oil to taste
- ☐ 2 garlic cloves
- ☐ 1 lb eggplant
- ☐ 3 ¼ cups short pasta (rigatoni, casarecce, rotini, penne)
- ☐ fine salt to taste
- ☐ ¾ cup salted ricotta cheese
- ☐ ¼ cup fresh basil leaves

METHOD

1. Wash and dry the cluster tomatoes, then cut them into quarters. Pour a drizzle of oil into a pan and sauté 2 peeled whole cloves of garlic, then remove them. Pour in the tomatoes and cook covered over very low heat for about 20 minutes.

2. When ready, blend them in a blender, transfer them to the pan, season with salt and cook for another 15 minutes.

3. Wash the eggplants, trim them, then cut them into thin slices. Fry the eggplants in abundant extra virgin olive oil heated. As they turn golden brown, drain and transfer them to a plate lined with a paper towel to absorb the excess oil. Season with salt to taste and set them aside.

4. Meanwhile, cook pasta in plenty of salted water.

5. Add the drained pasta into the pan, add fried eggplants, and fresh basil leaves and mix well to flavor.

6. Transfer the pasta onto serving plates, top each portion with salted ricotta cheese grated, and serve!

Cal serving: Kcal: 569 | Carbs: 77.4g | Fats: 21.2g | Prot: 17.1g | Fiber: 7.9g | Chol: 26.5mg

PREP 5 MIN

COOK 20 MIN

SERVES 4

INGREDIENT

- ☐ ⅔ cup red onion
- ☐ 1 ⅓ tsp fresh chili pepper
- ☐ ¼ cup black olives
- ☐ ¾ cup "fior di latte" mozzarella cheese
- ☐ extra-virgin olive oil to taste
- ☐ 3 ¼ cups peeled tomatoes
- ☐ 1 ½ tbsp salted capers
- ☐ fine salt to taste
- ☐ oregano to taste
- ☐ 11 oz whole grain spaghetti pasta

Cal serving:
Kcal: 404
Carbs: 54.2g
Fats: 13.6g
Prot: 16.3g
Fiber: 9.7g
Chol: 12mg

SPICY PASTA

METHOD

1. Cut the onion, chili pepper, and olives into thin slices.
2. Drain the mozzarella and cut it into small pieces.
3. Boil a pot full of salted water.
4. While the water is boiling, pour the olive oil into a frying pan and heat it over medium heat. Add the onion and red pepper and brown them.
5. At this point, pour in the peeled tomatoes and lightly crush them. Add the olives, capers, and salt, and cook the sauce for about 12 minutes on low heat. When the sauce is cooked, add the mozzarella and fresh oregano.
6. As soon as the water boils, pour the spaghetti into the pot and cook for the time indicated on the package.
7. Drain the pasta, transfer it directly to the pan with the sauce and toss with a ladle of the cooking water.
8. Plate and serve immediately! Enjoy!

PREP 35 MIN

COOK 20 MIN

SERVES 4

SEAFOOD SPAGHETTI

INGREDIENT

- [ ] 2 ¼ lbs clams
- [ ] 2 ¼ lbs mussels
- [ ] ⅔ lb squid
- [ ] 8 scampi
- [ ] ¾ lb spaghetti
- [ ] ⅔ lb cherry tomatoes
- [ ] extra-virgin olive oil to taste
- [ ] 1 garlic clove
- [ ] 3 tbsp white wine
- [ ] black pepper to taste
- [ ] fine salt to taste
- [ ] 1 small bunch parsley

METHOD

1. Remove broken or empty-shelled clams. Shake the remaining clams in the sink, healthy ones will remain closed. Rinse clams in a colander over the bowl. Add coarse salt, and soak for 2-3 hours to remove sand.
2. Meanwhile, remove the dirt from the shells of the mussels and remove the byssus: their filament.
3. Clean the squid by removing the head, guts, and outer skin. Open them and cut them into strips.
4. Now clean the scampi. Using scissors, cut off the sides of the tail, then remove the shell covering the abdomen. With a toothpick remove the black vein on the back of the langoustine.
5. Wash the tomatoes, cut them into wedges, and keep them aside.
6. Heat 2 tablespoons of olive oil in a large pot and, when hot, pour in the clams and mussels. Cook them over high heat covered for about 3 minutes, until they open completely.

7. Remove the mussels and clams, discard their shells, and set them aside. Keep the cooking liquid aside as well.

8. Add 2 tablespoons of extra virgin olive oil and a clove of brown garlic in a pan. Then place the squid in the pan, add a pinch of salt, and cook for 5 minutes. Finish by adding white wine to the pan to deglaze and cook until the alcohol has evaporated.

9. Remove the garlic, add the cherry tomatoes and cook for another 5 minutes.

10. Add the scampi and season with salt and pepper.

11. Meanwhile, cook the spaghetti in boiling water. Halfway through cooking, transfer the spaghetti to the pan with the squid. Continue cooking in the pan, adding the cooking liquid from the mussels and, if necessary, a little cooking water from the pasta.

12. Finally, add the shelled mussels and clams. Season with chopped parsley, plate and serve. Enjoy!

Cal serving: Kcal: 589 | Carbs: 75.1g | Fats: 13.3g | Prot: 40.6g | Fiber: 3.3g | Chol: 267mg

 For more information on how to cook pasta see the tips in the "Pasta Cooking Tips" section at the beginning of the chapter.

LEMON POTATOES

 PREP 15 MIN   **COOK 40 MIN**   **SERVES 4**

INGREDIENT

- [ ] 2 ⅔ lbs potatoes
- [ ] juice of 2 lemons
- [ ] ⅓ cup extra-virgin olive oil
- [ ] fine salt to taste
- [ ] rosemary to taste
- [ ] thyme to taste
- [ ] lemon wedges to garnish

METHOD

1. Preheat oven to 445°F in static mode and line a baking sheet with baking paper.
2. Peel the potatoes then cut them into 8 wedges and transfer them to a bowl.
3. In another bowl, combine the juice of two lemons, the oil, and a pinch of salt and emulsify with a whisk or fork.
4. Pour the emulsion over the potatoes and mix well.
5. Transfer the potatoes to the lined baking sheet, and add the rosemary and thyme.
6. Bake in the oven for 35 to 40 minutes.
7. Halfway through cooking, stir the potatoes.
8. Remove from the oven and serve the lemon potatoes accompanied by lemon wedges.

Cal serving: Kcal: 276 | Carbs: 63g | Fats: 0.3g | Prot: 7.4g | Fiber: 6.6g

MUSHROOM RISOTTO

PREP 15 MIN   COOK 30 MIN   SERVES 4

INGREDIENT

- ☐ 14 oz porcini mushrooms
- ☐ 2 tbsp extra-virgin olive oil
- ☐ 1 garlic clove
- ☐ fine salt to taste
- ☐ black pepper to taste
- ☐ 1 yellow onion
- ☐ 2 tbsp butter
- ☐ 4 ¼ cups vegetable broth
- ☐ 1 ¾ cup carnaroli rice
- ☐ 3 ¼ tbsp grated Parmigiano Reggiano DOP cheese
- ☐ 2 spoonfuls parsley

Cal serving:
Kcal: 540 | Carbs: 72.6g | Fats: 21.5g
Prot: 14.1g | Fiber: 4g | Chol: 49mg

METHOD

1. With a knife, remove the base of the mushrooms, then gently rub the cap with a damp cloth. Cut them vertically into slices about 1/4 inch thick.

2. In an oiled skillet, sauté a clove of crushed garlic. Add the sliced mushrooms and sauté over high heat for about 10 minutes. Season with a pinch of salt and pepper.

3. Finely chop the onion. In a saucepan, melt the knob of butter, add the onion and let it cook on low heat for 10-15 minutes, adding a ladle of broth if necessary.

4. Add the rice and toast it for a couple of minutes. When the rice has become almost transparent, add one ladle of broth at a time, stirring often. When the liquid is absorbed, add the next ladle of broth.

5. Add the porcini mushrooms and finish cooking.

6. When cooked, add a knob of butter and the grated Parmesan cheese and mix well. Plate, garnish with fresh chopped parsley, and serve!

PUMPKIN RISOTTO

PREP 20 MIN   **COOK 50 MIN**   **SERVES 4**

INGREDIENT

- ☐ 1 ½ quart vegetable broth
- ☐ 3 ½ oz yellow onions, chopped
- ☐ ⅓ lb pumpkin
- ☐ 1 ¾ tbsp extra-virgin olive oil
- ☐ 1 ¾ cups carnaroli rice
- ☐ ¼ cup white wine
- ☐ salt to taste
- ☐ black pepper to taste
- ☐ ¼ cup butter
- ☐ ¾ cup Parmigiano Reggiano DOP cheese

Cal serving:
Kcal: 541 | Carbs: 69.8g | Fats: 21.8g |
Prot: 14g | Fiber: 1.7g | Chol: 49mg

METHOD

1. First, prepare the vegetable broth. Cut the vegetables and put them in a large pot. Cover them with water, and add salt. Cover the pot with a lid and bring it to a boil. When it boils, lower the temperature and cook for about an hour over medium-low heat. Strain the broth and keep it warm.

2. Clean the squash, cut it into slices, and then into small cubes.

3. In a large skillet pour the oil, add the chopped onion and sauté over low heat. When it has softened, add the squash and sauté it for a few minutes, stirring occasionally. Add a ladleful of broth at a time until the squash is cooked (about 20 minutes).

4. Heat another large skillet. Add the rice and toast it for about 2 to 3 minutes, turning it often to avoid burning. When it completely changes color, add the white wine and let it fade while continuing to stir.

5. Transfer the rice to the pan with the pumpkin and stir well. Add one ladleful of hot stock at a time, waiting for the rice to absorb it all before adding the next ladleful. (It will take 15-20 minutes for the rice to cook completely.)

6. Season with pepper and salt and turn off the heat. Add butter and grated Parmesan cheese and stir to coat. Plate and serve immediately!

MOROCCAN-STYLE COUSCOUS

PREP 25 MIN

COOK 2 HOURS

SERVES 4

INGREDIENT

- [ ] 6 oz couscous, precooked
- [ ] 1 sachet saffron
- [ ] 1 pinch salt

FOR THE STUFF

- [ ] 2 ⅔ lbs leg of lamb (the flesh), cut into chunks
- [ ] 3 ½ oz white onions, peeled and sliced
- [ ] 1 oz fresh ginger, grated

- [ ] 2 zucchini, chopped
- [ ] 1 carrot, peeled and chopped
- [ ] 1 oz raisins
- [ ] 2 oz precooked chickpeas
- [ ] chopped parsley to taste
- [ ] extra-virgin olive oil to taste
- [ ] fine salt to taste

FOR THE BROTH

- [ ] leg of lamb (the bone)
- [ ] 1 stick cinnamon
- [ ] 1 carrot, peeled and cut into pieces
- [ ] 3 ½ oz white onions, peeled and sliced
- [ ] fine sea salt to taste
- [ ] black pepper to taste
- [ ] water

METHOD

1. Place the lamb leg bone in a high-sided pot. Add a cinnamon stick, carrot pieces, onion slices, black pepper, and salt.
2. Pour in 2 quarts of cold water, bring to a boil and cook for 40 minutes, removing the foam if necessary.
3. When the broth is ready, strain it through a strainer and keep it aside.
4. In a large oiled skillet, pour in the onion and ginger, and stew, blending with a ladle of broth if necessary. Let it cook for 10 minutes.

5. Add the lamb meat, season with salt, and pour in the hot broth.
6. Cover with the lid and let it cook for 30 minutes.
7 Add the zucchini, carrots, and precooked chickpeas. Season with salt and cook covered for another 20 minutes, adding the raisins 5 minutes before the end of cooking time.
8. Spread the couscous in a baking dish, creating a thin layer. Add the salt and saffron and pour in about 1 cup of hot broth until the couscous is completely covered.

Cover the dish with plastic wrap and let it sits for about 3 minutes until it has absorbed all the broth. Once the broth is completely absorbed, remove the foil and shell the couscous with a fork.
9. Serve by arranging the couscous at the base of the plate. Arrange the lamb pieces and vegetables on it and sprinkle with chopped parsley. Serve and enjoy hot!

Cal serving:
Kcal: 491
Carbs: 39g
Fats: 12g
Prot: 56.6g
Fiber: 7.8g
Chol: 177mg

MEDITERRANEAN STYLE POTATOES

PREP 10 MIN   COOK 40 MIN   SERVES 4

INGREDIENT

- ☐ 2 lbs potatoes
- ☐ 3 garlic cloves
- ☐ 3 Tbsp salted capers
- ☐ ¾ cup pitted black olives
- ☐ 7 oz red onions, sliced
- ☐ 1 cup tomato pulp
- ☐ 1 tsp fine salt
- ☐ black pepper to taste
- ☐ 4 Tbsp extra-virgin olive oil
- ☐ 1 tsp oregano

Cal serving:
Kcal: 244,5 | Carbs: 49.4g | Fats: 3g |
Prot: 12.3.g | Fiber: 5.7g

METHOD

1. Preheat the oven to 375°F in fan mode.
2. Rinse the potatoes under running water, then dry them and cut them into wedges without removing the skin.
3. Transfer them to a bowl and season with the peeled garlic cloves, desalted capers, black olives, onions, and tomato pulp.
4. Season with salt, pepper, olive oil, and oregano, and mix everything together.
5. Pour the contents of the bowl into a baking dish and transfer to the oven.
6. Bake for about 40 minutes, stirring every 10 minutes for even cooking.
7. Take the Mediterranean-style potatoes out of the oven and serve warm!

VEGETABLE COUSCOUS

PREP 25 MIN

COOK 15 MIN

SERVES 4

INGREDIENT

- ☐ 1 fresh chili pepper
- ☐ 3 ½ oz spring onions
- ☐ ½ lb eggplant
- ☐ ½ lb carrots
- ☐ ½ lb zucchini
- ☐ 3 ½ oz cherry tomatoes
- ☐ 1 garlic clove
- ☐ 3 ½ oz snap peas
- ☐ fine salt to taste
- ☐ 1 ¾ + ¾ tbsp extra-virgin olive oil
- ☐ ⅓ oz fresh ginger
- ☐ 5 ½ oz couscous, precooked
- ☐ 1 tsp powdered turmeric
- ☐ 1 ½ cup hot water
- ☐ mint, a few leaves

METHOD

1. Cut the chili pepper into strips, removing the seeds inside.
2. Wash and peel the vegetables.
3. Chop the spring onion.
4. Cut the eggplant into cubes, the carrots and zucchini into matchsticks, and the cherry tomatoes in half.
5. Heat a drizzle of oil in a large frying pan and sauté the chili pepper and whole peeled garlic clove.
6. Raise the flame and add the eggplant, spring onion, and carrots.
7. Season to taste for a few minutes, then add the peas and zucchini.

8. Season with salt and pepper to taste.
9. Remove the garlic and add the cherry tomatoes.
10. Cook for a few minutes, then turn off the heat.
11. Add the grated ginger and stir well to blend the flavors.
12. Pour the couscous into a large bowl and season with salt, turmeric, and olive oil.
13. Mix well, then pour in the water and cover the bowl with plastic wrap.
14. After a few minutes, the couscous will have absorbed all the liquid.
15. Fluff the couscous with a fork and plate it.
16. Add the vegetables on top of the couscous, garnish with a few fresh mint leaves, and serve.

Cal serving: Kcal: 251 | Carbs: 37.5g | Fats: 8.1g | Prot: 7.7g | Fiber: 7.4g

Did you know?

The name couscous refers to the famous semolina in very small grains that in North Africa is prepared at home and steamed in a saucepan called a *"cuscussiera"*.

Couscous is a dish of ancient Moroccan origin that over time has spread to many Mediterranean countries.

Not everyone knows that couscous is eaten with the hands by making small balls of semolina.

INGREDIENT

- [ ] 1 cup Manitoba flour
- [ ] 3 cups flour 00
- [ ] 1 tsp fresh brewer's yeast
- [ ] 1 cup water (at room temperature)
- [ ] 2 tsp fine salt
- [ ] semolina flour to taste
- [ ] 2 cups canned peeled tomatoes
- [ ] a drizzle extra-virgin olive oil
- [ ] a pinch oregano
- [ ] 1 lb buffalo mozzarella cheese or "fior di latte" mozzarella cheese
- [ ] fresh basil leaves

For more information on pizza, see the tips in the "Pizza Cooking Tips" section!

PIZZA

PREP 30 MIN **COOK 45 MIN** **SERVES 3**

METHOD

1. In a bowl, combine the two flours, add the crumbled yeast and a small part of the water. Mix, gradually adding the water a little at a time. After pouring in about half the water, add the salt as well. Knead by hand, gradually adding the remaining water.

2. When you have obtained a smooth dough, transfer the dough to a work surface and knead by hand until smooth and homogeneous.

3. Shape the dough into a ball and let it rise at room temperature for about 5 hours covered with a cotton cloth.

4. After the rising time has finished, start making the folds. Fold the dough over itself. Take one flap and fold it inward. Do the same thing with the flap underneath, then with the one on the left and the one on the right. Let the dough rest for half an hour and repeat. Do this for 3/4 times alternating folds and rise time.

5. The last time, close the dough by folding it inward and letting it rest for 2 hours covered with a cotton cloth.

6. After the 2 hours have passed, divide the dough into 3 and form 3 balls by closing each ball from the outside in. Let the balls rest for another 2 hours covered with a cotton dishcloth.

7. Preheat the oven to 480°F and dust the round baking sheets with a little durum wheat semolina flour.

8. With hands greased with olive oil, roll out the dough. Add a small amount of tomato pulp, a drizzle of olive oil, a pinch of salt, and oregano, place in the oven on the bottom shelf, and bake for 7 minutes.

9. At this point, if you wish, you can top the pizza with mozzarella cheese or your favorite toppings.

10. Change the oven mode to grill and bake the pizza on top of the oven for another 7 minutes. (Follow the same baking process for the other two pizzas).

11. Remove from the oven, cut into wedges and enjoy with friends!

Cal serving:
Kcal: 1679 | Carbs: 198g | Fats: 67.2g | Prot: 70.5g | Fiber: 103g

PIZZA COOKING TIPS

Choice of flour

1

A flour with a high protein content should be used for pizza preparation. In addition, each flour absorbs water differently. Therefore, depending on the flour mix used (strong flour, weak flour, whole wheat flour, etc.) it will consequently be necessary to change the amount of water used.

Amount of yeast and leavening

2

The less yeast you use, the more digestible the dough will be. You can use 1/3 teaspoon of fresh brewer's yeast and let the dough rise for 5 hours. If you do not have time, to decrease the rising time, increase the amount of yeast.

Absolutely forbidden!

3

it's forbidden to roll out pizza with a rolling pin! Pizza is rolled out with your hands. Spread the dough ball by making small holes with your fingers, first on one side and then on the other. Then spread the loaf with all the palms of your hands and enlarge the dough by helping with your fingers. The frame should remain thick.

Baking

4

The pizza should be baked in a wood-fired oven. But you can get an equally tasty pizza using a traditional electric oven. You just need to use a few tricks. Preheat the oven to the highest temperature in static mode. Arrange the pan with the pizza on the bottom and bake for 7 minutes. After that, switch to grill mode. Season the pizza and transfer it to the second rack. Switch to grill mode and cook it for another 6 minutes. When the crust starts to brown and the mozzarella starts to melt you can bake it.

Freezing

5

Pizza dough can be frozen after rising; it is best to divide it into portions and store it in freezer bags. Simply thaw the required portions at room temperature and proceed with the recipe.

CHICKPEA SOUP

INGREDIENT

- ☐ 10 ½ oz dried chickpeas
- ☐ 1 ½ quart vegetable broth
- ☐ 1 leeks
- ☐ ½ white onion
- ☐ 1 carrot
- ☐ 2 sprigs rosemary
- ☐ 2 bay leaves
- ☐ 3 tbsp extra-virgin olive oil
- ☐ 1 rib celery
- ☐ ¼ cup tomato puree (optional)
- ☐ fine salt to taste
- ☐ black pepper to taste

METHOD

1. Pour the chickpeas into a large bowl, cover them with water and let them rehydrate for at least 12 hours.
2. Drain and rinse the chickpeas, then set them aside.
3. Heat a pot of vegetable broth.
4. Meanwhile, remove the two ends of the leek, and cut it first vertically and then into thin slices.
5. Peel the celery and remove the outer, fibrous part with a vegetable peeler, then chop finely.
6. Peel and chop the onion and carrot.
7. Using kitchen twine, tie the rosemary and bay leaves to form a bunch.
8. Pour the oil into a saucepan, let it heat, and add the chopped celery, carrot, onion, and leek. Add a ladleful of hot stock and continue cooking for about 10 minutes.
9. Add the chickpeas, bay leaf, and rosemary bunch, and cover everything with the hot vegetable broth. Add the tomato puree, stir and cook covered over low heat for about 3 hours.
10. When cooked, remove the herbs and adjust the salt and pepper.
11. Plate the chickpea soup and serve it accompanied by croutons, slices of toast, or Greek pita bread. Enjoy!

Cal serving: Kcal: 356 | Carbs: 46g | Fats: 11g | Prot: 18.2g | Fiber: 12.4g

INGREDIENT

- ☐ 2 springs sage
- ☐ 2 spring thyme
- ☐ 2 spring rosemary
- ☐ 2 ½ lb pumpkin
- ☐ 1 lb carrots
- ☐ 4 Tbsp extra-virgin olive oil
- ☐ 1 shallot
- ☐ 4 cup water
- ☐ fine salt to taste
- ☐ ⅓ cup pumpkin seeds
- ☐ ½ cup sour cream
- ☐ black pepper to taste

Cal serving:
Kcal: 256 | Carbs: 19.7g | Fats: 17.1g
Prot: 5.8g | Fiber: 5.4g | Chol: 13mg

PUMPKIN AND CARROT VELOUTÉ

PREP 20 MIN   **COOK 1 HOUR**   **SERVES 4**

METHOD

1. Prepare the herb bundle by tying sage, thyme, and rosemary with a piece of twine and set aside.
2. Using a knife, remove the skin from the pumpkin, then divide it in half, and with a spoon scoop out the inner seeds. Cut the squash first into slices and then into cubes.
3. Peel and cut the carrots into rounds.
4. In a saucepan, pour the oil and heat it.
5. Chop the shallot, add it to the oiled pan along with the bunch of herbs, and brown for about 10 minutes.
6. Remove the herbs and add the squash and carrots. Season with salt and cook for 5 minutes, stirring occasionally. Then pour in the water and let cook covered for about 40 minutes.
7. Meanwhile, preheat the oven to 375°F.
8. Transfer the pumpkin seeds to a baking dish and toast them in the oven for about 15 minutes. Then set them aside.
9. When the soup has finished cooking, turn off the heat and blend with an immersion blender until smooth and homogeneous.
10. Distribute the velouté among the plates. Garnish with a spoonful of sour cream, some pumpkin seeds, and a pinch of black pepper. Enjoy your hot velouté on cold winter days!

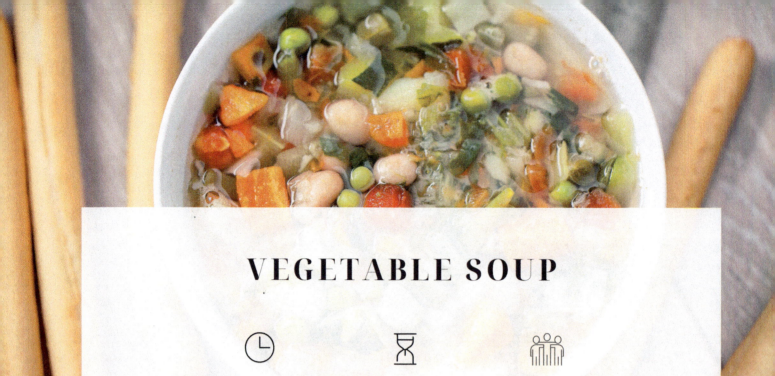

VEGETABLE SOUP

PREP 30 MIN   **COOK 50 MIN**   **SERVES 8**

INGREDIENT

- ☐ ½ lb pumpkin
- ☐ ½ lb borlotti beans
- ☐ 5 oz zucchini
- ☐ ⅔ lb cauliflower florets
- ☐ 5 oz leaks
- ☐ ¾ lb potatoes
- ☐ 1 lb cluster tomatoes
- ☐ 3 oz onions
- ☐ 3 oz carrots
- ☐ 2 oz celery
- ☐ ¼ cup extra-virgin olive oil
- ☐ 1 sprig rosemary
- ☐ 2 bay leaves
- ☐ ½ lb peas
- ☐ water to taste
- ☐ fine salt to taste

METHOD

1. Wash all the vegetables.
2. Peel the squash and remove the seeds and white filaments. Cut it into equal-sized slices and then into 1/2-inch thick cubes.
3. Husk the beans.
4. Peel the zucchini, then cut it into cubes.

5. Cut the cauliflower in half, remove the core, and cut the florets.

6. Peel the leeks then cut them into thin rings.

7. Peel the potatoes and cut them into cubes. Prepare the tomatoes: remove the stem, slice them, and cut them into cubes.

8. Peel and finely chop onion, carrot, and celery and keep aside.

9. Heat the oil in a large pot. Add the chopped carrot, celery, onion, and leek and sauté gently for about 10 minutes, stirring often. When the vegetables are golden brown, add the bouquet of rosemary and bay leaves and the beans and cover with a fingerful of water. Bring to a boil and cook for 2 minutes.

10. Add the squash, cover with a finger of water, bring to a boil, and cook for 2 minutes.

11. Add potatoes and cauliflower, cover with more water, and bring to a boil and cook covered for 25 minutes.

12. Add the zucchini, peas, and tomatoes. Add more water if needed, and season with salt and pepper. Bring to a boil and cook for another 2-3 minutes.

13. Remove the herb bouquet, plate, drizzle with a little oil, and serve the vegetable soup.

Cal serving: Kcal: 127 | Carbs: 20.7g | Fats: 2.8g | Prot: 5.1g | Fiber: 5.8g | Chol: 5mg

LEGUME AND BARLEY SOUP

PREP 15 MIN   **COOK 90 MIN**   **SERVES 4**

INGREDIENT

- ☐ 4 oz dried lentils
- ☐ 4 oz dried chickpeas
- ☐ 4 oz dried broad beans
- ☐ 2 oz dried borlotti beans
- ☐ 2 oz dried red kidney beans
- ☐ 2 oz dried cannellini beans
- ☐ 1 celery rib
- ☐ 1 carrot
- ☐ 1 white onion
- ☐ extra-virgin olive oil to taste
- ☐ 1 garlic clove
- ☐ 4 oz barley
- ☐ 1 bay leaf
- ☐ 1 ½ quart vegetable broth
- ☐ fine sat to taste
- ☐ black pepper to taste

METHOD

1. Soak all the dried legumes overnight.
2. Drain the legumes and rinse them under running water.
3. Heat the broth.
4. Meanwhile, clean and chop a celery stick, carrot, and onion and keep aside.
5. In a saucepan, heat a little oil. Add the mince and a whole clove of garlic and sauté for 5 minutes.
6. Pour in a ladleful of hot stock and continue cooking for another 5 minutes. Remove the garlic clove and pour the legumes, barley, and bay leaf into the pan. Stir well, then pour in the hot broth until all the vegetables are covered.
7. Cook over medium-low heat for about an hour and a half.
8. This hot soup is the perfect meal on a cold winter day!

Calories per serving: Kcal: 571 | Carbs: 82g | Fats: 13g | Prot: 31.5g | Fiber: 18.6g

CHICKPEA AND PUMPKIN SOUP

🕐
PREP 20 MIN

⏳
COOK 35 MIN

👪
SERVES 4

- ☐ 1 ⅓ lb delica pumpkin, cleaned
- ☐ 14 oz precooked chickpeas, drained
- ☐ 3 ½ oz chard

- ☐ 2 cups yellow onions
- ☐ 3 juniper berries
- ☐ 2 bay leaves
- ☐ 6 ½ cups water
- ☐ extra-virgin olive oil to taste

- ☐ fine salt to taste
- ☐ black pepper to taste

1. Peel and slice the onion.
2. Cut the pumpkin pulp into cubes.
3. Wash the chard and cut them into thin strips.
4. Pour the olive oil into a frying pan and heat it. Add the sliced onion and juniper berries and brown them. When the onion is golden brown, add the squash and sauté over medium heat.
5. Add the chickpeas, chard strips, bay leaf, salt, pepper, and water. Cook covered over medium-high heat for 15 minutes. After the 15 minutes have elapsed, remove the lid and continue cooking for another 15 minutes.
6. Remove the bay leaves and juniper berries.
7. Plate the soup, season with a drizzle of raw olive oil, and serve.

Note: Alternatively, you can blend it and serve it as vegetable puree.

Cal serving: Kcal: 150 | Carbs: 14g | Fats: 7.7g | Prot: 6.2g | Fiber: 9.7g

AUTUMN SALAD

PREP 10 MIN   -   **SERVES 4**

INGREDIENT

- ☐ 3 ½ oz arugula
- ☐ 2 Williams pears
- ☐ 3 oz Grana Padano DOP slivers
- ☐ 2 oz walnut kernels
- ☐ Extra-virgin olive oil to taste
- ☐ Fine salt to taste
- ☐ Balsamic vinegar to taste

METHOD

1. Wash and dry the arugula and pears. Place the arugula la in a bowl.
2. Cut the pears into wedges and remove the center part of the core. Cut the pear slices into very thin slices, pour them into the bowl with the arugula and toss gently.
3. Coarsely chop the walnuts and add them to the salad along with the grana slivers.
4. Season with salt, olive oil, and vinegar. Stir and serve!

Cal serving: Kcal: 281 | Carbs: 7g | Fats: 23.2g | Prot: 11.g | Fiber: 2.5g | Chol: 27mg

PREP 20 MIN

COOK 3 MIN

SERVES 6

INGREDIENTS

- ☐ 2 oz pine nuts
- ☐ 2 oranges
- ☐ 1 fennel bulb
- ☐ 1 oz raisin
- ☐ 1 tsp lemon juice
- ☐ 4 Tbsp olive oil
- ☐ a pinch of salt
- ☐ 1 tsp pumpkin seeds

FENNEL AND ORANGE SALAD

METHOD

1. Add pine nuts to a non-stick pan, toast them for a short period of time, then take the pan out of heat and place pine nuts aside.

2. Squeeze the juice from 1 orange and soak the raisins with the resulting juice for about 10 minutes.

3. Wash and dry the fennel bulb. Remove the stems, green barbs, and base. Cut it into 4 parts, then julienne it very thinly using a mandoline. Transfer it to a salad bowl.

4. Peel the other orange sharply, taking care to remove the white part. Cut it into thin slices and place it in the salad bowl.

5. Using a strainer, strain the raisins and transfer them to the salad bowl.

6. Pour the strained orange juice into a high-sided container. Add the lemon juice, oil, and a pinch of salt and blend with an immersion blender.

7. Pour the emulsion into the salad bowl, and mix well.

8. Add the pine nuts and pumpkin seeds, mix well, and serve.

Calories per serving: Kcal: 245 | Carbs: 11.6g | Fats: 19.4g | Prot: 6g | Fiber: 4.6g

WINTER SALAD

🕐
PREP 10 MIN

⧗
-

👪
SERVES 4

INGREDIENT

- ☐ 4 oz spinach
- ☐ 1 lb kaiser pears
- ☐ ½ lb precooked beets
- ☐ 4 oz walnut kernels
- ☐ 7 oz gorgonzola cheese
- ☐ extra-virgin olive oil to taste
- ☐ fine salt to taste
- ☐ balsamic vinegar to taste

METHOD

1. In a bowl, pour spinach and set aside.
2. Wash the pears and cut them into 4 wedges. Remove the core and peel. Cut the pears into 1-inch chunks and transfer them to the bowl with the spinach.
3. Cut the precooked beets into chunks and transfer them to the bowl.
4. Chop up the walnut kernels and add them to the bowl.
5. Take the gorgonzola cheese with a spoon and add it to the salad.
6. Season with salt, oil, and balsamic vinegar and toss to combine.
7. Your winter salad is ready to be served!

Calories per serving: Kcal: 512 | Carbs: 16.5g | Fats: 41.5g | Prot: 18.g | Fiber: 7g | Chol: 44mg

BAKED LAMB WITH POTATOES

 PREP 15 MIN COOK 90 MIN SERVES 4

INGREDIENT

- [ ] 2 ¼ lbs lamb
- [ ] juice of 1 lemon
- [ ] ⅓ cup dry white wine
- [ ] 5 juniper berries
- [ ] 1 garlic clove
- [ ] 2 bay leaves
- [ ] 4 sage leaves
- [ ] 1 spring onion
- [ ] 2 ¼ lbs potatoes
- [ ] 3 sprigs thyme
- [ ] 2 sprigs rosemary
- [ ] 1 cup water
- [ ] extra-virgin olive oil to taste
- [ ] salt to taste
- [ ] black pepper to taste

Cal serving: Kcal: 710 | Carbs: 39.9g | Fats: 40.6g | Prot: 42.9g | Fiber: 4.5g

METHOD

1. Place the lamb pieces back into a large bowl. Add the lemon juice, white wine, and crushed juniper berries, crushed poached garlic, bay leaves, and sage, and let the meat season for at least 30 minutes.

2. Wash and dry the spring onion, and trim off the root base. Cut it into strips lengthwise, then divide them in half.

3. Preheat the oven to 400°F in static mode.

4. Meanwhile, rinse the potatoes well under running water and dry them. Cut them in half and place them in a bowl. Add the spring onion and lamb with the seasonings (except garlic). Season with thyme and rosemary and cover with water. Season with olive oil, salt, and pepper, and stir to season.

5. Transfer to a baking dish and bake in the oven for about 1 ½ hours, taking care to cover the dish with aluminum foil halfway through cooking to prevent the meat from drying out too much.

6. Serve accompanied by rice pilaf or a side of vegetables.

PREP 10 MIN

COOK 15 MIN

SERVES 4

INGREDIENT

- [ ] 5 Tbsp breadcrumbs
- [ ] 3 sprigs thyme
- [ ] 1 lemon, juice, and zest
- [ ] 2 Tbsp flaked almonds
- [ ] fine salt to taste
- [ ] black pepper to taste
- [ ] 2 cod fillets
- [ ] 1 Tbsp extra-virgin olive oil

Cal serving:
Kcal: 236
Carbs: 11.4g
Fats: 12.6g
Prot: 19.4g
Fiber: 3.2g
Chol: 50mg

COD FILLETS IN CRUST

METHOD

1. Preheat the oven to 400°F in static mode.
2. In a bowl, combine the breadcrumbs, thyme, lemon zest, and juice.
3. Then add the slivered almonds, salt, and pepper and mix everything together with a spoon.
4. Using kitchen tweezers, remove any bones on the cod fillets. Lay the fillets on a flat plate and spread half of the olive oil and the almond breadcrumbs on top. Press down with your hands and make sure it adheres well on all sides of the fish.
5. Drizzle the bottom of an ovenproof dish with the remaining olive oil. Lay the breaded cod fillets inside the baking dish and add the rest of the breadcrumbs.
6. Bake in the oven for about 15 to 20 minutes. When a crispy crust forms on the surface, take the cod fillets out of the oven and serve them hot.

OCTOPUS AND POTATO SALAD

PREP 20 MIN

COOK 1 HOUR

SERVES 4

INGREDIENT

- [ ] 2 ¼ lbs potatoes
- [ ] 2 ¼ lbs octopus
- [ ] 2 bay leaves
- [ ] 1 bunch parsley
- [ ] ¼ cup extra-virgin olive oil
- [ ] ¼ cup lemon juice
- [ ] fine salt to taste
- [ ] black pepper to taste

METHOD

1. Wash the potatoes, then transfer them with all their skins to a saucepan and cover them with water. Cook for about 30-40 minutes from the time of boiling. They will be cooked when they are soft when pierced with a fork.

2. Meanwhile, clean the octopus. Turn and empty the head. With a small knife, remove the tooth that is in the center of the tentacles and remove the eyes.

3. In another pan, pour plenty of water, add the bay leaves and bring to a boil.

4. Dip only the octopus tentacles into the boiling water for a few moments and raise the octopus again. Do this 2-3 times, until the tentacles are well curled.

5. Submerge the octopus entirely in the water and cook it covered over moderate heat for about 50 minutes (Cooking time depends on the weight of the octopus).
6. Drain the potatoes and peel them. Dice them, transfer them to a bowl and keep them warm aside.
7. Wash and finely chop the parsley and keep it aside.
8. In a cooking bottle, pour the squeezed lemon juice, olive oil, salt, and pepper. Close the dispenser and shake the bottle.

9. Drain the pulp and let it cool for 10 minutes. Transfer it to a cutting board, cut off the head and detach the tentacles, then chop everything into small pieces.
10. Transfer the octopus pieces to the bowl with the warm potatoes. Season everything with the emulsion, flavor with chopped parsley, and mix with a spoon. Serve and enjoy!

Cal serving:
Kcal: 456
Carbs: 41.7g
Fats: 19.5g
Prot: 28.5g
Fiber: 4.1g
Chol: 162mg

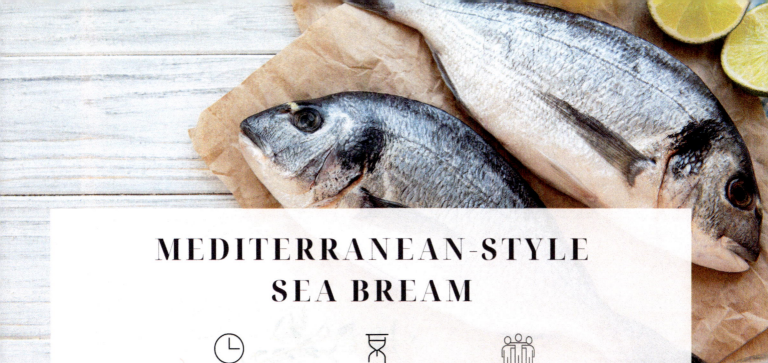

MEDITERRANEAN-STYLE
SEA BREAM

PREP 15 MIN   **COOK 30 MIN**   **SERVES 4**

INGREDIENT

- ☐ 2 sea bream, gutted
- ☐ thyme, to taste
- ☐ 2 garlic cloves
- ☐ fine salt to taste
- ☐ black pepper to taste
- ☐ 7 oz cherry tomatoes
- ☐ 1 Tbsp salted capers
- ☐ 1 cup pitted black olives
- ☐ 2 Tbsp extra-virgin olive oil

METHOD

1. Preheat the oven to 400°F.
2. Stuff the belly of the sea bream with fresh thyme, and 1 peeled garlic clove. Season the giltheads with salt and pepper and lay them on an oiled baking dish.
3. Wash the cherry tomatoes and slice them in half. Arrange them around the two giltheads in a baking dish.
4. Clean the capers by rinsing them thoroughly under running water to remove excess salt, place them on top of the giltheads.
5. Also, add the pitted black olives, and a few sprigs of fresh thyme and season with a drizzle of olive oil salt to taste.
6. Bake and cook the seabream for 25-30 minutes. Serve and enjoy!

Cal serving: Kcal: 234 | Carbs: 3.4g | Fats: 15.2g | Prot: 21g | Fiber: 1.6g | Chol: 63mg

INGREDIENT

- ☐ 3 lbs rabbit
- ☐ 1 onion
- ☐ ½ cup Taggiasca olives, pitted
- ☐ 1 sprig rosemary
- ☐ 1 glass red wine
- ☐ 2 cloves garlic
- ☐ 1 Tbsp thyme
- ☐ 5 Tbsp extra-virgin olive oil
- ☐ meat stock to taste
- ☐ 3 bay leaves
- ☐ fine salt to taste
- ☐ 2 Tbsp pine nuts

Cal serving:
Kcal: 428
Carbs: 7.1g
Fats: 17.9g
Prot: 30.3g
Fiber: 1g
Chol: 74mg

RABBIT LIGURIAN STYLE

 PREP 20 MIN   COOK 60 MIN   SERVES 6

METHOD

1. Cut the rabbit into many pieces, removing the head, liver, and kidneys.
2. In a large pot, heat olive oil on medium heat, add diced onions and minced garlic, and cook until translucent.
3. Add the rabbit pieces and brown them. Add the bay leaves, thyme (or marjoram) leaves, and chopped rosemary needles.
4. When the rabbit is golden brown, add a glass of red wine and let the alcohol evaporate.
5. Add the taggiasca olives and pine nuts and cook covered over low heat for about an hour, until the rabbit becomes tender (the meat should come off the bone easily). Occasionally add a ladleful of broth to the pot.
6. Plate the rabbit by drizzling it with plenty of cooking juices.

PREP 10 MIN

COOK 50 MIN

SERVES 4

INGREDIENT

- [ ] 8 Chicken drumsticks
- [ ] 3 Tbsp extra-virgin olive oil
- [ ] fine salt to taste
- [ ] black pepper to taste
- [ ] ½ glass of white wine
- [ ] 1 fresh chili pepper
- [ ] 2 cloves garlic
- [ ] 4 Tbsp capers in oil
- [ ] 7 oz red onions
- [ ] ¾ cup Gaeta olives pitted
- [ ] ¾ cup baked black olives
- [ ] ½ cup Greek black olives, pitted
- [ ] ⅓ cup water
- [ ] 1 ½ tomato puree
- [ ] 1 tsp dried oregano

Calories per serving:
Kcal: 521| Carbs: 6.9g | Fats: 34.4g
Prot: 43.4g | Fiber: 3.4g

MEDITERRANEAN STYLE CHICKEN THIGHS

METHOD

1. Place the chicken drumsticks in a bowl, season with oil, salt, and pepper, and set aside.
2. Slice the garlic and onion.
3. Heat a skillet and brown the chicken for 6 minutes per side. When it has a nice crust, add the white wine and let it fade. Transfer the chicken thighs to a plate and set aside.
4. Score the chili pepper, remove the inner seeds, and slice it thinly.
5. In the same pan in which you cooked the chicken, add the garlic, capers, olives, and onions. Sauté 2 minutes, then deglaze the bottom with water.
6. Pour in the tomato puree, add the thighs kept aside, and add salt to taste.
7. Cook covered over low heat for about 30 minutes.
8. Season with dried oregano and serve the chicken thighs hot.

INGREDIENT

- ☐ 1 tsp Cayenne pepper
- ☐ 2 tsp powdered turmeric
- ☐ 2 tsp smoked paprika
- ☐ 1 tsp cinnamon powder
- ☐ 2 tsp cumin
- ☐ 1 tsp coriander seeds, powdered
- ☐ fine salt to taste
- ☐ black pepper to taste
- ☐ 1 ¼ cup Greek yogurt
- ☐ 1 ¾ lb Chicken breast
- ☐ 1 cinnamon stick
- ☐ 3 pods cardamon
- ☐ 1-star anise
- ☐ 2 ⅔ cups water
- ☐ 1 white onion
- ☐ Fresh ginger to taste
- ☐ 1 fresh chili pepper
- ☐ 2 ¼ cups basmati rice
- ☐ 1 clove garlic
- ☐ 1 ¾ tbsp extra-virgin olive oil
- ☐ cilantro or parsley leaves

Cal serving:
Kcal: 686 | Carbs: 84.9g | Fats: 12.4g
Prot: 58.7g | Fiber: 3.7g | Chol: 129mg

CHICKEN CURRY

PREP 20 MIN   COOK 15 MIN   SERVES 4

METHOD

1. In a frying pan, pour in the spices and toast them over low heat for a few minutes. Transfer the toasted spices to a large bowl, add a pinch of salt and pepper and the Greek yogurt and stir to make a creamy mixture.

2. Cut the chicken breast into 1/2-inch cubes and place them in the marinade. Stir it all together, cover it with plastic wrap and let it marinate in the refrigerator for a couple of hours. Rinse the rice well and pour it into a saucepan. Add the cinnamon stick, cardamom pods, star anise, coarse salt, and water. Cover with a lid and bring to a boil. When it boils, lower the heat and let it cook for 10 minutes.

3. Meanwhile, slice or chop the onion. Grate the fresh ginger and chop the chili pepper, removing the stem but keeping the seeds.

4. Pour the oil into a pan, add the crushed garlic, onion, ginger, and chili and sauté lightly over medium heat. Add the chicken with all the marinade and let it cook for 10 minutes.

5. Finely chop the cilantro leaves, add them to the pan, and stir. Your chicken curry is ready to be served with basmati rice.

MEATBALLS WITH TOMATO SAUCE

PREP 30 MIN

COOK 20 MIN

PIECES 24

INGREDIENT

- ☐ 1 oz breadcrumbs
- ☐ ½ lb sausage
- ☐ ½ lb beef, ground
- ☐ fine salt to taste
- ☐ black pepper to taste
- ☐ 1 pinch dried oregano
- ☐ 1 tbsp parsley
- ☐ 1 pinch nutmeg
- ☐ ¼ cup Parmigiano Reggiano DOP cheese
- ☐ 1 egg
- ☐ extra-virgin olive oil to taste

METHOD

1. Cut the breadcrumbs into pieces, pour them into a blender and reduce them to crumbs.
2. Slit the sausages lengthwise and remove the casings.
3. Pour the sausage and ground meat into a bowl and mash them with a fork.
4. Add a pinch of salt and pepper, oregano, a pinch of grated nutmeg, chopped parsley grated Parmesan, chopped breadcrumbs, and egg. Mix with a fork, then knead with your hands until smooth.
5. Break off pieces of dough and form them into balls. You should obtain about 24 balls.
6. Heat the oil in a nonstick pan. When the oil is hot, lay the meatballs in it and cook them on both sides for a couple of minutes. Add the tomato pulp, water, and a pinch of salt, and cook for about 20 minutes.
7. Season with dried oregano and enjoy!

Cal serving: Kcal: 492 | Carbs: 20.7g | Fats: 34.9g | Prot: 23.7g | Fiber: 3.1g

SICILIAN-STYLE CHICKEN

PREP 10 MIN

COOK 50 MIN

SERVES 4

INGREDIENT

- ☐ ½ cup cherry tomatoes
- ☐ extra-virgin olive oil, to taste
- ☐ 2 cloves garlic
- ☐ 2 fresh chili pepper
- ☐ ½ cup black olives, pitted
- ☐ 3 ¾ Tbsp capers in vinegar
- ☐ wild fennel to taste
- ☐ 12 oz rose wine
- ☐ 12 oz water
- ☐ fine salt to taste

METHOD

1. Wash and dry the cherry tomatoes, cut them in half, and keep them aside.
2. Remove the stem from the chilies, cut them open to extract the seeds, and slice them thinly.
3. Heat the olive oil in a skillet, add the two cloves of poached garlic and the chiles and sauté for a couple of minutes.
4. Place chicken pieces in the pot, brown for 2-3 minutes on each side on medium heat.
5. Pour in the cherry tomatoes, olives, capers, and wild fennel.
6. Deglaze with the wine and let it evaporate.
7. Pour in the water and cook for 45 minutes over medium-low heat covered, stirring occasionally.
8. When the cooking is finished, remove the poached garlic cloves and adjust the salt if necessary. Serve hot and enjoy!

Cal serving: Kcal: 497 | Carbs: 4g | Fats: 31.7g | Prot: 37.6g | Fiber: 1.1g | Chol: 179mg

BEEF STEW

PREP 20 MIN   COOK 2 HOURS   SERVES 4
                  + 20 MIN

INGREDIENT

- ☐ 8 cups meat broth
- ☐ 1 sprig rosemary
- ☐ 1 sprig thyme
- ☐ 3 leaves sage
- ☐ 1 stalk celery
- ☐ 1 carrot
- ☐ 1 onion
- ☐ 2 lbs beef (or pork)
- ☐ 1 stick butter
- ☐ 4 tbsp extra-virgin olive oil
- ☐ sea salt to taste
- ☐ black pepper to taste
- ☐ 1 glass red wine

METHOD

1. Heat a saucepan with the meat stock.
2. Tie the thyme, sage, and rosemary with a piece of kitchen twine and keep aside.
3. Clean the celery, carrot, and onion, and finely chop the vegetables.
4. Cut the meat into 2-inch cubes.
5. Heat the butter and oil in a saucepan. Add the chopped vegetables and sauté for a few minutes.
6. Raise the flame, add the meat, and brown it. Season with salt and pepper, then add the red wine and let it reduce.
7. Add the herb bouquet, cover with the hot beef stock, and cook lid on medium heat for at least 2 hours.
8. When cooked, remove the herb bouquet, adjust the salt if necessary, and serve.

Cal serving: Kcal: 529 | Carbs: 9.7g | Fats: 29.9g | Prot: 49.6g | Fiber: 1.8g | Chol: 159mg

TUNA IN PISTACHIO CRUST

 PREP 10 MIN

 COOK 5 MIN

 SERVES 4

INGREDIENT

- [ ] 1 ¼ lb tuna
- [ ] 3 tbsp extra-virgin olive oil
- [ ] 3 tsp sun-dried tomatoes in oil, drained
- [ ] 5 tbsp pistachios, shelled
- [ ] 1 tbsp poppy seeds
- [ ] 2 tbsp breadcrumbs
- [ ] fine salt to taste

METHOD

1. Place the tuna steak in the freezer for at least an hour (this will make it easier to cut it). Cut it lengthwise into slices about 1 inch thick.
2. Arrange tuna slices in a baking dish, and drizzle with olive oil.
3. Chop the dried cherry tomatoes finely with a knife and transfer them to a bowl.
4. Add the chopped pistachios, poppy seeds, breadcrumbs, and a pinch of salt and mix well.
5. Coat tuna slices in breadcrumbs, pressing to adhere.
6. Heat a couple of tablespoons of olive oil in a frying pan over medium heat. Once hot, add the tuna slices and cook for 1 minute on each side to achieve a pink center.
7. Remove the tuna slices from the pan, slice them, and place them on a serving plate. Serve immediately.

Cal serving: Kcal: 413 | Carbs: 7.1g | Fats: 26.4g | Prot: 36.6g | Fiber: 3.3g

BAKED SALMON AND POTATOES

SECTION

PREP 10 MIN

COOK 50 MIN

SERVES 4

INGREDIENT

- ☐ 4 salmon fillets
- ☐ 1 ⅓ lb potatoes
- ☐ 1 tbsp white wine vinegar
- ☐ rosemary to taste
- ☐ thyme to taste
- ☐ salt to taste
- ☐ black pepper to taste
- ☐ extra-virgin olive oil to taste

METHOD

1. Preheat the oven to 400°F in static mode and line a baking sheet with baking paper.
2. Meanwhile, peel the potatoes and cut them into half-inch rounds. Transfer them to a bowl and season with olive oil, salt, thyme, and rosemary sprigs.
3. Mix well, then spread the flavored potatoes on the baking sheet and bake them in the oven for about 20 minutes.
4. Move the potatoes to the sides of the baking dish, lay the salmon fillets in the center, and season with salt to taste. Bake for another 15 to 20 minutes or so.
5. Your salmon with a side of baked potatoes is ready to serve.

Cal serving: Kcal: 394 | Carbs: 22.2g | Fats: 11.5g | Prot: 39.7g | Fiber: 3.3g | Chol: 52mg

CHAPTER 4 DESSERTS

SIMPLE & HEALTHY FOOD RECIPES

ZOE VALASTRO

BUTTERLESS SHORTCRUST PASTRY

PREP 15 MIN   -   SERVES 6

INGREDIENT

- [ ] 2 eggs
- [ ] 1 egg yolks
- [ ] 2 tbsp water
- [ ] ½ cup extra-virgin olive oil
- [ ] 1 ½ cup powdered sugar
- [ ] 4 ⅓ cup flour 00
- [ ] 1 ½ cup potato starch
- [ ] 1 tsp baking powder

METHOD

1. In a bowl, pour the whole eggs and yolk and beat with a whisk. Add the water and extra virgin olive oil in a trickle, continuing to beat.
2. Pour in the powdered sugar by sprinkling and incorporating it while stirring vigorously with the whisk. Sift the flour, potato starch, and baking powder into the bowl and mix by hand.
3. Once you have obtained a fairly solid mixture, transfer it to a pastry board and continue to work vigorously with your hands until you have obtained a smooth and compact dough ball.
4. Wrap the loaf with plastic wrap and allow it to rest in the refrigerator for about 1 hour.
5. You can use the shortcrust pastry to make a tart or cookies.

Cal serving: Kcal: 717 | Carbs: 105.1g | Fats: 24.8g | Prot: 18.4g | Fiber: 1.8g

PREP 30 MIN

COOK 50 MIN

SERVES 10

GRANDMA'S CUSTARD PIE

INGREDIENT

- ☐ Shortcrust Pastry without Butter (see the previous recipe)
- ☐ 4 ½ cups whole milk
- ☐ 1 egg yolks
- ☐ 3 eggs
- ☐ 1 lemon peel
- ☐ 2 cups sugar
- ☐ 2 ¼ tbsp cornstarch
- ☐ 2 tbsp flour 00
- ☐ 3 ½ tbsp pine nuts
- ☐ Powdered sugar to taste

METHOD

1. Start by preparing the shortcrust pastry using the "Shortcrust Pastry without Butter" recipe. While the shortcrust pastry rests in the refrigerator, prepare the custard.
2. Peel 1 lemon with a vegetable peeler, being careful not to peel the bitter white part.
3. In a small saucepan, pour the milk and add the lemon peel, and heat over low heat.
4. Meanwhile, in a bowl, break the 3 whole eggs and yolk, pour in the sugar, then mix the ingredients. When the sugar is absorbed, add the flour and cornstarch sifted through a strainer and mix well.
5. As soon as the milk starts to bubble, remove the saucepan from the heat and remove the lemon peel from the milk.
6. Pour some of the milk into the bowl with the egg and sugar mixture and stir well to dilute.
7. Put the pot of milk back on the heat and pour the mixture with the eggs into it. Continue to cook slowly, stirring the cream with a whisk for about 10 to 15 minutes.

8. Once ready, transfer the cream to a shallow, wide baking dish and immediately cover it with plastic wrap. Allow the cream to cool to room temperature.

9. Meanwhile, preheat the oven to 320°F in static mode and butter (or oil) and flour in a 10-inch diameter baking pan.

10. Take the shortcrust pastry, lightly flour the work surface and roll it out to form a disk 1/10 inch thick. Roll out the shortcrust pastry on a rolling pin and roll it out onto the baking sheet, being very careful not to break it.

11. Adhere the bottom and edges by pressing down with your fingers and discard the excess dough. Prick the bottom with the tines of a fork and pour in the custard.

12. Roll out the leftover pastry and unroll the disk onto the baking sheet to cover it. Remove the excess edges and bake in the oven for 50 minutes on the bottom shelf. Move the cream pie to the middle shelf and bake for 10 minutes at 355°F.

13. Take the cake out of the oven and let it cool fully. Sprinkle powdered sugar on top before serving.

Notes:

1. If you notice that the surface darkens too much during baking, you can cover it with aluminum foil.

2. You can freeze the leftover shortcrust pastry or use it to make cookies.

Cal serving: Kcal: 613 | Carbs: 87.8g | Fats: 23.7g | Prot: 12.3g | Fiber: 1.3g

CARROT CAKE

 PREP 30 MIN   **COOK 50 MIN** **SERVES 6**

INGREDIENT

- ☐ 10 oz carrots
- ☐ 3 eggs
- ☐ 1 cup sugar + powdered to taste
- ☐ 1 pinch fine salt
- ☐ ½ vanilla pod
- ☐ 3 cups flour 00
- ☐ 3 tsp baking powder
- ☐ ½ cup almond flour
- ☐ ½ cup sunflower seed oil

METHOD

1. Preheat the oven to 350°F in static mode.
2. Peel the carrots, then grate them finely. Place them in a fine-mesh strainer set over a bowl and gently crush them with a spoon so that some of their liquid is expelled.
3. In a bowl, pour the eggs, sugar, and a pinch of salt and whisk together with electric whips until smooth.
4. Slit the vanilla pod lengthwise and extract the seeds by scraping them out with a small knife. Add the vanilla seeds to the mixture.
5. Mix the flour, baking powder, and almond flour together in a different bowl, use a spoon or sifter to distribute it evenly.

6. Operate the whisks and add the powders one tablespoon at a time.

7. With the whisks running, slowly pour in the oil and continue working the mixture until it becomes thick and smooth.

8. Finally, add the grated carrots and gently stir the mixture with a pastry spatula, incorporating the carrots into the batter.

9. Butter and line a rimmed cake pan and pour the batter inside.

10. Bake for 45 minutes, then take it out of the oven and let it cool completely in the mold before unmolding.

11. Dust the cake with powdered sugar and serve.

1. Note: For a more fragrant cake, you can add the juice of an orange or cinnamon powder to the batter.

Cal serving:
Kcal: 548
Carbs: 77g
Fats: 21.9g
Prot: 10.7g
Fiber: 3.7g
Chol: 102mg

WINE COOKIES

PREP 30 MIN **COOK 25 MIN** **PIECES 40**

INGREDIENT

- ☐ 1 tbsp anise seeds
- ☐ ⅔ oz white wine
- ☐ 2 ½ cups flour 00
- ☐ ½ tbsp baking powder
- ☐ 1 ¼ cup sugar
- ☐ 1 pinch fine salt
- ☐ 1 cup vegetable oil
- ☐ sugar to taste

METHOD

1. Preheat oven to 350°F in static mode and line a baking sheet with baking paper.
2. Pour the anise seeds into the white wine and set aside.
3. In a bowl, pour the sifted flour, baking powder, sugar, and a pinch of salt. Mix, then make a hole and pour the oil and wine with the anise seeds inside. Knead with your hands.
4. Transfer the dough to the work surface and compact it well. Break off a piece of dough about 1 oz at a time and knead it with your hands until you have an 8-inch long loaf.
5. Roll it up by joining the ends together and making them fit tightly. Then press one side of the cookie onto the sugar. Continue with the same process until you run out of dough. You should get about 40 cookies.
6. Arrange the cookies on the prepared baking sheet, taking care to turn the sugared side upward. Bake for about 25 minutes, then take them out of the oven and let them cool before serving.

Cal serving: Kcal: 97 | Carbs: 15.6g | Fats: 2.8g | Prot: 1.5g | Fiber: 0.3g

ALMOND CRUNCH

PREP 5 MIN   COOK 15 MIN   SERVES 6

INGREDIENT

- ☐ 3 ⅓ cups blanched almonds
- ☐ ½ cup acacia honey
- ☐ 1 ¾ cup sugar
- ☐ lemon juice

METHOD

1. Preheat the oven to 375°F static mode and line two baking sheets with baking paper.
2. Pour the peeled almonds onto one of the baking sheets and toast them for a few minutes in the oven.
3. Pour the honey, sugar, and a few drops of lemon juice into a steel pan and stir well, melting them over medium heat.
4. Check the temperature with a kitchen thermometer. Once the temperature reaches 285°F, pour the roasted almonds into the pan with the still-warm honey and stir well.
5. When the temperature reaches 340°F, take the pot off the heat and pour the mixture into the lined baking pan, using a wooden spoon to spread it evenly.
6. Allow the almond mixture to cool down to room temperature, once cooled, cut it into bars on a cutting board.

Cal serving: Kcal: 528 | Carbs: 48g | Fats: 31g | Prot: 13g | Fiber: 6g

PANNA COTTA (COOKED CREAM)

 PREP 5 MIN　　 **COOK 15 MIN**　　 **SERVES 3**

INGREDIENT

- ☐ ½ oz gelatin
- ☐ 1 vanilla bean
- ☐ 2 cups heavy cream
- ☐ 6 ⅓ tbsp sugar

Cal serving:
Kcal: 351
Carbs: 26g
Fats: 25.9g
Prot: 3.6g
Chol: 85mg

METHOD

1. Let the gelatin sheets sit in cold water for 10-15 minutes.
2. Cut the vanilla pod lengthwise and scrape out the seeds with a knife.
3. Combine cream, sugar, vanilla seeds, and pod in a saucepan, and heat over low flame.
4. Once it boils, turn off the heat, and remove the pod with kitchen tongs.
5. Drain softened gelatin and add to hot cream mixture, stirring until fully dissolved.
6. With a ladle, pour the panna cotta into 4 molds with a capacity of 5 ounces each.
7. Transfer the molds to the refrigerator and let them rest for at least 5 hours.
8. Dip the molds for a few seconds in boiling water to unmold them perfectly.
9. You can serve the panna cotta with caramel, melted chocolate, or fruit coulis.

Eating is a necessity.
Eating intelligently is an
Art
- F. de La Rochefoucauld

Conclusion

We hope you were able to execute all the recipes, and especially that you enjoyed them.

As we said at the beginning of the book, the Mediterranean diet, it's not just a diet but it's a real lifestyle, so it can be followed by anyone, both adults, and children.

As you may have noticed, the Mediterranean diet is rich in tastes, and flavors. If you make it your own and make it a real lifestyle you will notice how your life will change for the better! Not only will you be able to lose weight, if this is your goal, but your health will benefit!

It is scientifically proven that those who follow a Mediterranean diet have longer lives and fewer health problems.

Take some time to dedicate to cooking these dishes. Choose Mediterranean dishes over the usual fast-food options. Not only will you eat much healthier dishes, but they will also taste better! This will allow you to gain health and also save money.

Below is what your meal plan could look like. We are sure that after that experience you will not be able to do without the Mediterranean diet!

MEAL PLANNER - WEEK 1

	BREAKFAST	LUNCH	SNACK	DINNER
MON	Fig Crostini 1 coffee 1 glass orange juice	Vegetable Soup	5 almonds	Cod Fillet in Crust + Salad
TUE	Cantucci (Almond Cookies) 1 cup milk 1 coffee	Mediterranean Pasta + Mediterranean Style Chicken Thighs	1 fruit	Pumpkin and Carrot Veloutè
WEN	Apple Cake 1 coffee	Mediterranean Style Sea Bream + Lemon Potatoes		Winter Salad
THU	Cantucci (Almond Cookies) 1 cup milk 1 coffee	Chikpea Soup	1 fruit	Piadina Romagnola
FRI	Baked Eggs in Tomato Sauce	Mushroom Risotto	1 fruit	Baked Salmon and Potatoes
SAT	Fig Crostini 1 coffee	Octopus and Potato Salad	1 fruit	Pizza
SUN	Soft Lemon Cake 1 coffee	Moroccan Style Couscous	Panna Cotta	Caponata + 1 slice toasted bread

MEAL PLANNER - WEEK 2

	BREAKFAST	LUNCH	SNACK	DINNER
MON	Cantucci (Almond Cookies) 1 cup milk 1 coffee	Legume and Barley Soup	Zucchini Rolls	Mediterranean Style Chicken Thighs + Salad
TUE	Yogurt Cake 1 coffee	Meatballs with Tomato Sauce + Salad / Spinach / Green Peas	1 fruit	Autumn Salad
WEN	Fig Crostini 1 coffee	Pumpkin Risotto + Sicilian Style Chicken		Vegetable Soup
THU	Cantucci (Almond Cookies) 1 cup milk 1 coffee	Chicken Curry	1 fruit	Rabbit Ligurian Style + Lemon Potatoes
FRI	Fig Crostini 1 coffee	Chickpea and Pumpkin Soup		Beef Stew + Salad
SAT	Apple Cake 1 coffee	Stuffed Mozzarella	1 fruit	Bari Style Focaccia
SUN	Cantucci (Almond Cookies) 1 cup milk 1 coffee	Seafood Spaghetti + Tuna in Pistachio Crust	Grandma's Custard Pie	Baked Lamb with Potatoes

MEAL PLANNER - WEEK 3

	BREAKFAST	LUNCH	SNACK	DINNER
MON	Fig Crostini 1 coffee 1 glass orange juice	Legume and Barley Soup	5 almonds	Bruschetta
TUE	Apple Cake 1 coffee	Spaghetti with Tomato Sauce + Meatballs	5 almonds	Winter Salad
WEN	Baked Eggs in Tomato Sauce	Piadina Romagnola	1 fruit	Pumpkin and Carrot Veloutè
THU	Cantucci (Almond Cookies) 1 cup milk 1 coffee	Chikpea Soup	1 fruit	Mediterranean Style Sea Bream + Lemon Potatoes
FRI	Fig Crostini 1 coffee	Spaghetti with Clams + Fennel and Organge Salad	5 almonds	Mediterranean Style Chicken Thighs + Salad
SAT	Cantucci (Almond Cookies) 1 cup milk 1 coffee	Octopus Salad + Mediterranean Style Potatoes	1 fruit	Pizza
SUN	Soft Lemon Cake 1 coffee	Vegetable Couscous	Wine Cookies	Cod Fillet in Crust + Salad / Spinach / Green Peas

MEAL PLANNER - WEEK 4

	BREAKFAST	LUNCH	SNACK	DINNER
MON	Yogurt Cake 1 coffee	Mushroom Risotto + Rabbit Ligurian Style	Stuffed Figs	Vegetable Soup
TUE	Fig Crostini 1 coffee	Chikpea Soup	Zucchini Rolls	Baked Salmon and Potatoes
WEN	Cantucci (Almond Cookies) 1 cup milk 1 coffee	Chicken Curry		Autumn Salad
THU	Fig Crostini 1 coffee	Mediterranean Pasta + Mediterranean Style Chicken Thighs	Hummus + Vegetable Sticks	Caponata + 1 slice toasted bread
FRI	Cantucci (Almond Cookies) 1 cup milk 1 coffee	Beef Stew + Salad	1 fruit	Eggplant Rolls + Salad / Spinach / Green Peas
SAT	Apple Cake 1 coffee	Stuffed Mozzarella + Salad / Spinach / Green Peas		Bari Style Focaccia
SUN	Cantucci 1 cup milk 1 coffee	Seafood Spaghetti + Tuna in Pistachio Crust	Almond Crunch	Winter Salad

INDEX

INDEX

Have you enjoyed this book?

If you found this book useful and enjoyed it, please leave a review on Amazon. We appreciate it very much!